Golden Nuggets
For This Thing Called Life

I0616890

Wykinnya Whitehurst

Golden Nuggets For This Thing Called Life

Copyright © 2023 *Wykinnya Whitehurst*

All Rights Reserved

No permission is given for any part of this book to be reproduced, transmitted in any form or means; electronic or mechanical, stored in a retrieval system, photocopied, recorded, scanned, or otherwise. Any of these actions require the proper written permission of the author.

Dedication

This book is dedicated to all the people I love, care about, and who love and care about me. To my family members that I have loved and lost; My sister Katrina, my mother Janet, my father Samuel (squirrel), my great Grandparents Eunice and Harvey Blake, and my Grandparents May and Lee Stovall. Godmother Elsie, God Sister Pam, and Cousin Charlene Sims, Uncles and Aunts Howard Lee, Anne Perl, Susie, Luster, James, Obey, Calvin, and all those who have positively impacted my life.

Acknowledgments

I would like to thank God for the abilities and gifts He has bestowed upon me. I can do all things through Him which strengthens me. To my loving and supportive husband, Eric, thank you for being being wonderful in all things us, and beyond, and I love you. I'd like to thank my support system (they know who they are), for keeping me grounded and moving forward. Thank you to my Auntie Louise, my beautiful daughters, my loving son, my grandchildren, family members, and friends for their contributions to my life and this journey.

About The Author

I have known Wykinnya Whitehurst for over 15 years. Her passion for helping people reach their personal goals and aspirations is huge! Although she is the same sweet, energetic, and giving woman I have always known, she has also grown so much over the years. This growth is apparent through her writing, as she openly shares with the reader through a daily quote.

There is no better teacher than one who has experienced the lesson firsthand. Wykinnya is a teacher, but she is also teachable, which are two great attributes to have. She took the "nuggets" from her own personal life and poured them over the pages in this book so she could help inspire, motivate, and show you that you are not alone. Each day you can read a page and it will either relate to you or someone you know. If you are having a hard time maneuvering through life, open the book and read the quote for that day. If you are having a fantastic time in your life, open the book and read a passage to stay grounded. This is a book for everyone!

I hope that you enjoy reading this book as much as I did. Wykinnya's words will ignite a fire and bring the person that may be buried deep inside of you to the surface where she/he is meant to be.

Kimberly Alease Bell

January 1

Take a look at your life and notice the good things. When you do, it is a guarantee that you will get more of those good things. To complain, waddle, and be ungrateful is a guarantee that you will have more of the same. There's always something in your life to be grateful for, no matter what it looks like. If you dig deep enough, you can find it. If you're reading this book today, you can be grateful that you have eyes to see. So there you have it; be grateful for the little things in your life, and I promise you, you'll get more of the same.

Notes:

January 2

Whenever we try to do things our way, that's when we really miss it, because we don't know what we're doing. That is why we make mistakes. The same mistakes over and over and over again. Eventually, we remember God, and ask Him to order our footsteps. This is when the game and everything changes for the better.

Lord, help me to always put You and Your will first in my life. Help me learn how to honor You in all that I do. The steps of a good man are ordered by the LORD: and he delighteth in his way. Amen! Psalm 37:23 King

Notes:

January 3

Meeting people where they are has been one of the most difficult lessons I've had to learn. We're used to doing things our way, and when others don't seem to get it, we tend to judge them right away. Let me tell you, you weren't always where you are now.

We must be patient with others, especially with those we love, because God is patient with us. So, before you pass judgment on others for not being where you are, remember that you were once that person who needed someone to be patient with you. You are not perfect, and you should not judge others as if you are.

Notes:

January 4

Don't let the actions of others dictate your future behavior. When you are a good person at heart, all you want to do is help others. People will be people; they are who they are, and they will remain so until they see the need to change. Don't give up and don't let the negative behaviors of others change who you are? God has bestowed upon you the gifts of compassion, love, and companionship. The enemy is out to find, kill, and destroy the person God created you to be, but he can only win if you let him. Don't let the ways of the world determine who you are.

Notes:

January 5

We don't have the power to change other people; but we can choose not to be present for the bad behavior of others. As the old cliché goes, when you're sick and tired of being sick and tired, things change. Now, if you haven't been sick and tired yet, you will continue to do what you're doing and continue getting what you're getting.

But, rest assured, there will come a time when you will say to yourself, "I've had enough this is over!" People cannot treat you any kind of way unless you allow them. Yes, you can influence how others treat you, but not how they behave. You can only walk away from the person in the situation and tell yourself, "I am better than this." Understand WHO you are and WHOSE you are. You are the King's daughter and son, the most High God. Act Like It!

Notes:

January 6

Holding on to pain and hate is like walking around all day carrying a 1,000-pound person on your back. Try not forgiving someone if you want to be attached to them forever. Forgive someone who has hurt you if you want to be free of them. Moving forward requires letting go of the past; you can't move forward while looking in the rearview mirror. I'm here to tell you that the person who hurt you is living their life. They are not thinking about you or how they have harmed you. Just let it go. It is liberating and will allow you to move forward.

Notes:

January 7

If you have someone in your life that is professing to love you, but all they seem to do is hurt you, that's not love. Love doesn't hurt, it's gentle, kind, patient, loving, and endearing. When someone becomes arrogant, disrespectful, hurtful, and mean, you have entered into something different. It's definitely not love. It's abuse. If someone is If someone is abusing you in any way (verbal, physical, or emotion-ally), it's time to walk away. This is not a healthy relationship for you, or for the person that's abusing you, and if you have children it is unhealthy for them too. It is a poison that can and will kill if you allow it. Love is not abuse.

Notes:

January 8

You walk into a room and the energy shifts. It seems as though everyone has gone quiet. Nine times out of ten, it's because you're bringing a certain type of energy into that space. And it's not a good energy. People are not always talking about us behind our backs. We must get out of the notion that everyone is against us and be open to meeting and interacting with new people, ideas, and places. Take a look in the mirror and ask yourself: "Is it me against me and not necessarily the world against me? How can I open myself up in a more positive way?"

Notes:

January 9

We must all be the change we want to see in the world because the world will not change on its own. To make a difference in the world, everyone must do their part. It's pointless to speculate on what people should, could, or would have done. Teach me what to do and when to do it, Jesus. I know I frequently miss the mark, therefore I need your assistance to become the person I aspire to be.

Notes:

January 10

God has implanted an internal alarm clock within each of us as women. This alarm sounds when some-thing is wrong, and our Spirit indicates that something isn't quite right. We could often save ourselves a lot of trouble, heartache, and pain if we had just listened to that intuition and the small, still voice of God saying, "Beware! There's danger ahead!" Instead, we want what we want and choose to ignore His voice and go in the opposite direction of where He wants us to go. I implore you to pay attention to what your Spirit is trying to tell you when you sense something is off. I guarantee that if you listen, it will save you in the end.

Notes:

January 11

When you love someone, you shouldn't sit around wondering if he or she loves you back. If you have to question someone's love for you, they're not doing it right. If you have to question your feelings for someone, something is wrong. There should never be any doubt about love. When you love someone, you show them through your actions and words. If you truly love someone, it should be simple to say, "I love you." Show people that you care about them by everything you do and say. Make a concerted effort to be an example of what you're saying to others.

Notes:

January 12

Live by faith not by sight 2 Corinthians 5:7. What exactly does that mean? We all have some faith. That is why we fantasize about going to school or getting married. We aspire to own a business or going to school. Dreaming is simply believing in something that you cannot see or touch; it is intangible. Faith is believing in something despite the fact that you cannot see it. All you need is a small amount of faith, as small as a mustard seed. That's all you need - just a smidgeon of fear will lead you to places you don't want to go, so let a speck of faith overcome any fear that is keeping you from dreaming and moving forward.

Notes:

January 13

Be wary of coveting what others "appear" to have. When we see other people doing great things in the world, it may appear that everyone else is growing and progressing, but we are stagnant. It's not because you're being punished or because God loves them more than you. The truth is that we have no idea what other people have gone through to get to where they are today. What is meant for you is meant for you, and what is meant for them is meant for them. Maybe it's just not your season. Simply be patient. Have a little faith that God will grant your heart's desires. Don't be concerned about what the Joneses are up to acoss the street because the grass isn't always greener on the other side. Instead of admiring other people's lawns, I encourage you to water your own. Be grateful for the simple things in your life because when you begin to be grateful for what you have, God will bless you with more.

·

Notes:

January 14

We've all heard the saying, "Everyone that goes with you, can't stay with you." This is absolutely correct. We're all in different stages of life. I don't want what my friends want, and vice versa. I don't want a bunch of Kinnya's walking around, and I consider myself to be a pretty good woman: God-fearing, honest, hard-working, compassionate, caring, and all that jazz. But, to be honest, there are some places I'm going where others cannot accompany me. Just as you can't take me some of the places you're going, and that's fine. People who are currently in your life serve a purpose. There are people who have been in your life all your life, and then there are those who come and go. If they aren't already gone, they will be soon. It is critical that you distinguish between the temporary and permanent people in your life. When it's time, let go of the temporary or seasonal people; don't cling to them. We never want to cling to someone or something that God is telling us to let go of.

Notes:

January 15

The very thing that you're holding onto is the thing you need to let go of. Life is a perpetuating circle, so whatever goes around comes around. What you give is what you get. A closed fist never gets the thing it wants in it. If this is you, and you've been holding onto something tightly because you are afraid that if you give it away you won't have it anymore. Ask God for His help and His guidance, and He will give you what you need. If we could do it all by ourselves, we would not need God's help. Open your mouth, get on your knees, start praying and ask God to help you. I promise you, as soon as you ask for His help, He's going to help you. He's going to dispatch His angels to help you, but first you have to ask.

Notes:

January 16

Take on the goal of improving yourself by all means necessary. Take heart and resolve to do good. Take a position for what you believe in, and do your best to be a walking, talking example of that belief. Until you take a leap of faith and give something a try, you'll never know how good you could be. Failure is merely a stepping stone to success. Raise yourself up and start over. Don't lose hope because of your own pessimism.

Notes:

January 17

What you tell yourself is impactful. Exactly what are the stories you tell yourself? Are you trying to better yourself? How well do you encourage yourself? Do you feel like you're giving yourself the power you need? Your words have the power of life or death, and once you say a thing, you can't take it back. Therefore, it is essential that you choose them carefully, even when speaking to yourself. So, if you're criticizing yourself about about how stupid you are because you never do this or that, I have some bad news: You will never follow through on anything; but if you speak words of life into yourself — "I can," "I will," and "I should" — then nothing or no one will ever be able to bring you down, not even yourself.

Notes:

January 18

Those around you are unable to read your mind or predict what you are thinking or about to say. You must speak up and request what you want or need. It's absurd to think that someone else is aware of your innermost thoughts and feelings, especially if you have not voiced them. That is not how things work in the real world. You have a voice. Use it!

Lord, help me to be brave enough to ask for what I want and need. I don't wish to be afraid of what I presume will be the response. Help me to live with strength and courage rather than fear and intimidation. AMEN!

Notes:

January 19

If you want different results, you need to try new approaches. Doing something over and over again and expecting a different outcome is the definition of insanity. Okay, so they're right. That's true for every one of us, but when we finally decide that we've had enough, we open the door to new possibilities. The prospect of change often causes worry and can be scary. In fact, nothing is scarier than staying stuck in beliefs that no longer work for you. The ability to shift one's perspective is the most potent tool at our disposal. Make up your mind today that your own way of thinking, being, responding, and reacting is no longer acceptable. Tell yourself, "As of today, I have changed my mind. I will no longer be held hostage by my thinking."

Notes:

January 20

In this life, each and every one of us will experience a wide range of highs and lows, good things and bad things, victories and defeats. There are essential nuggets and tidbits concealed inside the throes of each encounter. Having the ability to overcome any challenge demonstrates that one has taken full advantage of all that life has to offer.

Lord, there is nothing I can do without your covering and protection. I don't want to do this life without you by my side. AMEN!

Notes:

January 21

Before passing judgment on others, think. Don't make a decision until you have all of the facts, and even then don't pass judgment. It's easy to become engrossed in conversations about other people. Remember that kindness always comes back to the giver threefold. If we don't have anything positive to add to the conversation, let's keep our mouths shut.

Lord, help me to ignore destructive conversations. Assist me in detecting hidden messages in small talk that bring people down. Jesus, teach me to stand out and not blend in. Amen!

Notes:

January 22

God has strategically placed people in your life to help push you to the next level. We don't always recognize it when it's happening; in fact, sometimes we don't recognize it until it's too late, but there are those who are there to help push you forward. Nobody gets through life by themselves. When God created Adam, He said it was not good for him to be alone, so He created Eve. Genesis 2:18. What makes you believe you are any different from the first two humans on the planet? People do not just happen to enter our lives. Everyone who crosses your path serves a purpose.

Notes:

January 23

Have you ever wondered why God put your eyes in the front of your body? Well, it's so that you can move forward. So, did you put one foot in front of the other today? He did not place one of your eyes behind your back. His design was on purpose, not an accident. Keep looking forward. You will not make it to your destination looking behind you. Consider it in this way. Everything you need and use regularly is right in front of you. So, if you want to get somewhere, you should always be staring straight ahead.

Notes:

January 24

Anyone who wants more from you than you are willing to give is attempting to take advantage of you. Life should be a game of give-and-take rather than always giving and never receiving. People who take all the time and never give of themselves are selfish and greedy. God did not create us in this way. Give of yourself, your love, and your peace for this is the way God intended.

Notes:

January 25

People can say pretty much anything to you. The manner in which they interact with you, on the other hand, is crucial. In what ways do they show their concern for you? In today's society, the phrase "I love you" is thrown around carelessly. However, such words are meaningless unless they are backed up by action. If you pay attention to a person's actions rather than their words, you can save yourself a great deal of emotional and mental anguish.

Notes:

January 26

Your gift is the thing in your life that you do the best with the least amount of effort. It may be more than one gift at times. God bestows gifts on each of us for His plan and purpose for our lives. If you don't know what your gifts and talents are, you should get down on your knees and ask God what He has instilled in you. Believe me when I say that there is only one person on the planet who can do what you can do in the way you can do it. So, don't covet what your neighbor or friend has. "You shall not covet your neighbor's house; you shall not covet your neighbor's wife, or his male servant, or his female servant, or his ox, or his donkey, or anything that is your neighbor's" (Exodus 20:17 ESV).

Notes:

January 27

One of the most valuable gifts you can give to another person is your appreciation. We enjoy hearing what we mean to those around us. We all love giving and receiving love and kindness. Want to get rid of some people in your life? Take advantage of their generosity and kindness, and you will always lose them every time.

Notes:

January 28

I'll be the first to admit that I have no idea what I am doing in my own strength. I can accomplish anything with God's help. It is in our best interest to consult God if we want the best results for our future. He is fully aware of what is going to happen. He can see the finish line before the race begins. Don't misunderstand me! Because of the unpredictable nature of life, things do not always go as planned. The road God has for you is the road for you,regardless of whether or not there are obstacles along the way.

Notes:

January 29

What is meant for you is meant for you, and what is meant for me is meant for me. There is no one alive who can keep you from fulfilling your God-given destiny. If something is meant to be for you, it will be. You don't have to worry about there not being enough of anything; there is. Consider it this way. If you don't get your portion, it's because it wasn't meant for you in the first place. Unlike us, our God keeps His promises, and He says what He means and means what He says. He never vacillates between truth and untruth. If He has given you a vision and a dream for it, it is yours. All you have to do is stay put and wait on His timing rather than yours.

Notes:

January 30

We have the power to choose what consumes our thoughts. You can combat any negative thought with a positive one. We have more power over our lives than we think. Don't get me wrong! I am not speaking of other people and their behaviors because we have no control over anyone else's actions. But when it comes to our actions and thoughts, it's totally on us.

When I am tempted to dwell on self-defeating or negative thoughts, may I instead contemplate your goodness and mercy. I want to stop worrying about things outside of my control and instead enjoy and concentrate on the good in my life. AMEN!

Notes:

January 31

We are a reflection of what we think, believe, and feel. The paradox of wanting to be free from something while thinking in a way that prevents us from achieving that freedom keeps us bound and enslaved. My forefathers were able to sing despite experiencing what can only be described as hell on earth. They focused their...their thoughts and dreams on what might happen in the future rather than what was happening in the here and now. We are all capable of achieving the same goal. You can create the future you want by thinking about it, believing in it, and experiencing it in the present.

Notes:

February 1

You can only help others to the extent that you are able. When we think about the well-being of our family and friends, our hearts break. However, the unfortunate reality is that we are powerless to save the world. Only those who seek and desire our assistance are deserving of it. This is our job. When we start wanting things for others more than they want for themselves, it becomes about us rather than them, which can lead to frustration and disappointment.

Lord, I pray that I may be a source of blessing and assistance to those whose care you have entrusted me with. Help me recognize when I've had enough and need to let go. I never want to be an impediment to anyone seeking your assistance, guidance, or advice.

Notes:

February 2

No one said this life we've been given would be easy. "To whom much is given, much is required," says Luke 12:48. Every adversity contains lessons, wisdom, and understanding to help us get through it. Remember this when life's challenges seem insurmountable or depressing. We cannot progress if we refuse to learn the lessons that life has to offer. So take up your cross and know that no matter how small the steps are, they are steps forward, and you will never be given more than you can handle.

Notes:

February 3

Like everything else, life has its ups and its downs. Your kindness and compassion will mean everything to someone who is going through a difficult time. Any act of kindness, no matter how small, can have a significant impact. Don't say or do anything if you can't bring life to the situation.

Lord, teach me how to speak to others in your way. Help me understand what to say, when to say it, and how to say it. I want to move in response to your prompting, not my own.

Notes:

February 4

I don't need to be right in someone else's eyes to be whole or complete. As long as I know something without a shadow of a doubt, I am good with that. Someone else agreeing with me doesn't validate or invalidate me. Who does it matter to most that you are right? Would you rather prove a point or keep the peace? There may be times we feel as though our opinions are what matter most, when in fact, it is relevant only to us. There is no price you can put on having peace of mind and peace in your home. Is it worth it to always be right?

Notes:

February 5

Prayer really does change things. If you think for one moment that your prayers are meaningless to God and have fallen on deaf ears, think again. In human form, our prayers are a direct line of communication with our Creator. You were created full of purpose and with a plan. The only reason I am where I am today is because my grandmothers prayed for me. The greatest part was when I developed a relationship with God for myself. I then learned how to pray for others as well as for myself, which has manifested my faith, hope, dreams, aspirations, and purpose.

Lord, help me to pray when times are good and bad. Help me to not forget who and what You are. Help me to grow in you and your word. Teach me to become a house of prayer, and to never take You for granted. AMEN!

Notes:

February 6

Sometimes our relationships can feel like we're treading water. Relationships can reach a stalemate at times. They don't appear to move forward or backward; they just exist. We frequently forget that relationships require effort. The same things that got us here will not always be the same things that keep us going. Be creative and reinvent yourself and your relationships. Keep an eye on the temperature of those relationships and decide whether it's worth fighting for or if the season has ended. Know that when the season changes, weather will follow.

Lord Jesus, I'm sick and tired, of me. Please help me in energizing my life and relationships. Help me to step outside of my comfort zone and take risks that will propel me forward in my purpose and lives of those assigned to me. AMEN!

Notes:

February 7

You give, you get, you reap, you sow. It is un-avoidable and inevitable. So, be very careful how you treat other people. It comes back magnified and amplified threefold. So, before you do what you have been contemplating, but haven't carried through yet, ask yourself: What are the ramifications of my actions? Is it worth it? For there is always a reaction to every action.

Lord, I want to make good decisions that are designed to help, not to cause harm. Teach me the errors of my ways and to be responsible in what I do. AMEN!

Notes:

February 8

People are just that, people. They are not the be-all and end-all of our lives. They are simply people. When we look for people to play god-like roles in our lives, we are bound to be disappointed. There is no one on this planet who can complete you. That is God's job and God alone. The people in our lives can and will, hopefully, enhance the life we have. However, they are incapable of filling the void that only God can. So, when you feel lost and incomplete, seek guidance and answers from your creator, not from man.

Notes:

February 9

For many of us, our childhoods were less than ideal, but we are no longer children. There comes a time in our lives when we must move on and accept responsibility for the lives we now lead. Make the choice to either rise up or continue to fall short. Dig deep and pull out what is burning inside you — telling you there is more to life than where and what you are doing currently. Follow God and not your heart, for the heart can be deceitful and pull the wool over your eyes.

Notes:

February 10

Good friends are often happy when you are happy, sad when you are sad, and weary when you are weary. However, your success will not be shared by everyone. Some people may even rejoice in your anguish. Moving up in life can endanger those closest to you. They may believe that as you mature, they will lose their place in your life. As a result, they try to keep you confined to your current situation. This is their problem, not yours. Refuse to be complacent because others perceive your growth as a threat. Those who are meant to accompany you on your journey will do so no matter what.

Notes:

February 11

Life is a blessing. Each day, each morning, you have an opportunity to open your eyes, to hear and do for yourself. The beauty in life is that you get one. Think about it. So many people did not wake up this morning. Some do not have jobs to go to. We mess up when we turn our blessings into burdens. The very thing we asked God to do, we complain about every morning when that alarm clock goes off. So many people are praying for the very thing we take for granted each day.

Notes:

February 12

What's holding you back? There is no guarantee that you will be able to do anything that you put off today for tomorrow. There is no better time than now to do everything you can in the next 24 hours to move ahead in the world and in the life God has planned for you. When God asks you, "what have you done with the time I have given you?" What will your story line consist of?

Lord, show me how to live my life in the way you want me to. I want to follow where you lead, not go my own way. Help me hear your voice and to do what you say.

Notes:

February 13

The distinction between failure and growth is that failure, when viewed through disappointed eyes, provides nothing to look forward to. Looking at growth through the lens of failure, in contrast, teaches us a different way of being and doing, achieving, and reaching. It is a stepping stone of life. Without falling, we have no idea what it takes to pick ourselves back up and the strength we will gain in doing so. Strength is often buried within the weaknesses of our footsteps. But remember without the fall, we will never know where that strength lies.

Notes:

February 14

You are where you are at this time, this season, and this point in your life, on purpose. The path you may have taken to get here may not have been planned, but the journey still led you to where you needed to be. Everything has a reason and a season. Embrace where you are, remain open to guidance, and seek the subtle nudges from God directing your path to the next steps, toward the next phase, and into the next chapter of your life.

Lord Jesus, help me to embrace the season that I am in and the grace to endure all that it has to offer. AMEN!

Notes:

February 15

Whatever is needed for you to move forward in any project, job, or relationship, God will provide. He is moving people, places, and things to get you exactly where you need to be. Pay attention to what He is showing you. Hear His still, small voice, and He will send what or who is needed in that time and season. Be open and vulnerable enough to accept help from those who are strong when you are weak.

Lord Jesus, teach me to seek assistance from those who are capable and willing to assist me in my hour of need. I know that pride gets me nowhere, and I don't want to carry it because it is a hindrance to who I am and the direction I'm going.

Notes:

February 16

You are a moving billboard and business card. What you have and what has been instilled within you radiates outward. Don't work so hard at trying to get others to accept you. People will react to who and what you are on the inside. Only those in need of what you have to offer will see and be drawn to the light that shines within. Relax! You are not required to pursue. They will arrive in due course.

Lord Jesus, teach me to be confident in who You created me to be. Sometimes I feel anxious and in-secure. Help me to hold on to You and never let You go. AMEN!

Notes:

February 17

Predators prey on the frailties, insecurities, and weaknesses of their victims. They will take until there is nothing left. They will make you feel guilty for things they have done or are doing. They have a way of making their victims feel inferior to them. Their primary goal in a person's life is to destroy. If you aren't careful and seek the face of God, they can and will win every time.

Notes:

February 18

When you change your mind about something, it changes everything. A new life necessitates a new min-dset, a new focus, new goals, and to be honest, some new people. Growth requires new beginnings, new strengths, and a new attitude. It is the foundation for success. In the words of my dear friend, "Nothing changes if nothing changes."

Lord Jesus, as I walk through changes and growth, I know that you will be with me. Assist me in accepting changes and new opportunities that come my way. I place my trust in you and only you. AMEN!

Notes:

February 19

Are you pulling on doors that God has closed? There are some doors that no man can open, and some that no man can close. God is the one that can do either. Oftentimes, these doors are disguised as our prayers when we have asked Him to move in our lives. But we forget that God is unlike any man, and He moves in His own time and in His own way. The thing we prayed about, He answered. It just may not have been the answer we were seeking. If the purpose is to control the narrative, then leave God out of it because it will never end up the way you think it should. God is God all by Himself, and he doesn't need our help.

Notes:

February 20

It goes against the nature of God to try to force people to stay in your life that must leave. Those that are meant to stay will stay, and those who are not will leave. Holding on to things that God is trying to free us from goes against God's plan. Some people have a temporary status. Trying to convince yourself other-wise can be detrimental to your spirit, your life, and your world. Let them go. Seasonal people are just that: they will pass through. Permanent people are in it for the duration with no convincing to stay required.

Notes:

February 21

What do you stand on when times are hard? Hide scripture in your heart to recite in tough times because God's word is living and active; it never ceases to deliver. When needed, it will be there. Hide the word in your heart, and it will never leave you uncovered and no one can take it from you. When life is dark, and you're in despair, it will bring you to a place of peace, understanding, and comfort.

Jesus, Lords, I want to learn your word. Show me how to keep it hidden in my heart so that I can use it at all times. Even if things don't go my way, I don't want to be left without your protection.

Notes:

February 22

Anger turned inward is depression. When depress-sion sets in, it clouds your perception of things. It whispers sweet nothings in your ear, telling you how useless and worthless you are. It separates you from those that love and care about you. Oftentimes, we turn on the ones we love the most, unaware of how to manage the pain, anger, and fear we are experiencing. Seek the necessary help in times you are no longer able to deal with hardships you've been given. Needing and asking for help has never been associated with weakness. The weakness is not asking for help when you need it.

Notes:

February 23

Knowledge is power. Not acknoledgeing the man in the mirror doesn't make him invisible. You will never fix what you refuse to see. If you can't see it, then maybe your perception is distorted. Remove the blinders, and more will come into focus.

Lord Jesus, guide me in making essential changes in my life. Help me to change the things in my life that I can and accept the things that I cannot. Help me to learn something fresh from each experience that I can apply in the future. AMEN!

Notes:

February 24

Are you settling for less than God's best? We cannot jump on the first thing that comes our way; we need guidance and clarification on what, when, and where. Looks can be deceiving, and when we fail to see what is right before our eyes, the fallout can, oftentimes, be detrimental. God knew us before we were formed in our mother's womb. He knew we would turn right when He explicitly told us to turn left. He knew our ending before our beginning. So, it is wise to seek His guidance in ALL decisions, no matter big or small, because ultimately God's plan is what's best.

Notes:

February 25

What is your deepest desire? The thing that keeps you awake at night? That thing that, no matter what you do, keeps coming to the surface? It is your destiny that is calling. It can be postponed, but not denied. You can't keep it under control or contain it. In this case, the options are straightforward. Relax and let God's will be done, or go against the grain and fight until there is no more fight left. But ultimately, destiny will prevail.

Lord Jesus, I want to fulfill all the plans you have for me. I'm tired of spinning my wheels and getting nowhere fast. I can't do this without you. AMEN!

Notes:

February 26

Good deeds and hard work never go unnoticed by God. He knows and sees all things. Don't become consumed with what the world says or thinks, about you. In the end, God has the final say. Keep doing the right things for the right reasons, and your rewards will be just. Stand strong in your efforts and know that God and God alone sits on the throne

Lord Jesus, sometimes it is hard to accept that what we do goes unnoticed and unappreciated by others. I don't want to be affected by the actions or inactions of others. AMEN!

Notes:

February 27

Avoidance has never been the key to unlocking anyone's true potential or allowing them to step into their life's predestined path. To tame the lion, you must first enter the ring with him. Only then will you have the greatest chance at success. On the other side of fear, and uncertainty is where our opportunity for breakthrough lies. The only thing stopping us from progressing is ourselves. We can live fearlessly as long as we have God's grace.

Notes:

February 28

Only you can decide how your life will go. Nothing can stop you from fulfilling the plan God has for your life. Don't allow people to take your power. People are unable to take anything that you do not offer.

Lord Jesus, teach me how to make the best choices for my life. I don't want to live a life of regret and despair but one of joy and fulfillment.

Notes:

March 1

Treat others in the same manner that you would like to be treated. God can elevate from the bottom to the top, and from last to first. Therefore, you should exercise extreme caution in how you deal with the people that you consider to be irrelevant. They might one day turn out to be the people you need.

Lord Jesus, teach me to value individuals regardless of their social standing. The last thing I want to do is treat some people better than others. To you, each one of us is indispensable. Help us learn to place as much value in others as you do in us. AMEN!

Notes:

March 2

God's grace and mercy is what keeps us going and sustain us in difficult times. It is impossible to earn His grace; rather, it is freely given. Not because of who we are, but because of the nature of who He is. Once we are able to grasp that analogy, we are able to appreciate how His kindness endures across time and eternity.

Lord Jesus, your grace and kindness are more than enough for me. Even if I had a thousand tongues, they would not be enough to express how much I love You and appreciate everything You've done. So I give thanks to the unchanging God that you are. AMEN!

Notes:

March 3

One day, one step at a time. We must spend each day concentrating on what is in front of us. Looking to today in pursuit of tomorrow's solution results in redundancy. Nobody can guarantee what will happen tomorrow. Be in the moment you are in.

Lord Jesus, help me to treasure every moment of every day. Not being concerned about what tomorrow may bring. I don't want to waste my time worrying about problems that haven't happened yet or an-ticipating circumstances that may never happen. Teach me to appreciate my moments rather than squander them. AMEN!

Notes:

March 4

Our hearts can be filled with happy or negative emotions, which both have consequences. It has major implications for us. Easily losing one's temper when things aren't going our way is a trait of young children. However, a winners' tactics involve pushing through painful feelings. You can never lose if you keep your head on straight and your thoughts uncluttered.

Lord, help me to control my emotions in difficult situations. It's not who I aspire to be, but I try to avoid having to making snap judgments. No matter how trivial the topic may seem to me, I want to run it by you first. I need your counsel always Lord. AMEN!

Notes:

March 5

God cares about the things we care about. What concerns us concerns Him. He knows our innermost desires and thoughts. Call out to Him, surrender to His will, and He will always direct your path. Ask for His will, and it shall be given.

Lord Jesus, let everything in my life be according to Your will and not mine. I mess things up immensely when I put my will before yours. You are the one who knows what I need. Let your will be done in my life. AMEN!

Notes:

March 6

As long as we live on this earth, there will be disappointments. Things will happen, and people will let you down. This doesn't mean we should sit around and wait for dissapointments to happen. Find the positive in your life and focus on that because what you focus on and give your attention to will grow.

Lord Jesus, please enable me to overcome any situations that do not produce positive outcomes. Please help me accept both the good and the bad and find contentment in them. AMEN!

Notes:

March 7

The battle is not yours, says the Lord. Every fight that knocks at your door is not an invitation to indulge. Trouble can't exist on its own; it requires a willing participant. There are times the very best thing we can do for ourselves is to turn away. It is just that simple; turn away, let go, and let God.

Lord Jesus, because you created me you know that I want to help everyone. I know that this is not my job but Yours. Teach me to release those things into Your hands that are out of my control. AMEN!

Notes:

March 8

Feel the fire within you that says, "You can, you will, you are good enough." It is a glimpse of your purpose. If it is in your heart to transform the world and the worlds of those around you, you can prepare to take to the skies, and God will be the wind beneath your wings.

Jesus, you have placed inside of me a burning desire to be a change maker for this world. Give me the grace to stand in what and who I am . So that I might be able to face all that comes my way. AMEN!

Notes:

March 9

What we allow in our lives will persist. When people treat you unkind, and show disrespect, take notice. They are showing you who they are. There is nothing you can do to change that. The best and only thing you can do is to become unavailable for that behavior because disappointment without action is acceptance.

Lord, help me to always appreciate myself and to refuse to accept terrible behavior from others. I understand that pleasing You requires me to be kind to myself, which means walking away from people, places, and things that are not guiding me to my destiny. AMEN!

Notes:

March 10

We are all puzzle pieces in life. Each element is being deliberately organized by God. Each piece has a certain purpose and cannot be moved. Connected puzzle pieces neatly fit into position. Pay attention since an imposter, like an extra puzzle piece may try to sneak in and usurp the role of the original piece.

Help me Jesus, to discern what is real from what I perceive to be real. I don't always know or com-prehend what's going on in other people's hearts and and their intentions. Please grant me strength and wisdom in this area of my life. AMEN!

Notes:

March 11

Be mindful of the words you speak over your life. What you pour into your system and spirit will always come out. Telling yourself what you aren't and what you can't have will manifest. Garbage in, garbage out. Likewise, when you tell yourself what you can and will have, it will flourish.

Lord Jesus, I want to speak life over myself. I want to not only be able to lift up those around me but to lift up myself as well. Teach me how Lord. AMEN!

Notes:

March 12

Not doing something because we don't feel like it is not a legitimate excuse to not do it. It pushes everything else for that day back, in essence, making more work for the days to come. Procrastination is the recipe for laziness. Be very careful what you put off today for tomorrow. "The soul of the sluggard craves and gets nothing, while the soul of the diligent is richly supplied." Proverb 13:4

Lord Jesus, teach me to be a valuable contribution to you, my family, friends, and my church. I want to accomplish the tasks that have been allocated to me enthusiastically, rather than sluggishly or apprehend-sively. AMEN!

Notes:

March 13

Forgiving others for their wrongdoings is the best thing we can do for ourselves. It is not about who's right or wrong but our ability to move through and past the hurt and pain of disappointment. Just as God has forgiven our wrongdoings, we must show the same mercy to others. Remember, what goes around will come around. Things that have been done to us have a boomerang effect; it always comes back to its place of origin.

Notes:

March 14

There are some things in this life that are unavoidable. It can be delayed, yes, but never denied. We all have an individual journey that requires specific people, places, and things along the way. It will encompass challenges, battles, victories, and losses. It is part of the cross that each of us has to bear. But the Lord gives us no more than we can handle. He will strengthen us over and over again, allowing us to come out on the other side of adversity.

Notes:

March 15

At the end of the day, the only ones who care whether we are right is ourselves. So why do we try to persuade others that our point of view is the only one that is correct? Our physical selves are always driven to prove themselves. In reality, we devote our time and energy to the wrong things and attempt to satisfy the wrong people. The only thing that truly matters at the end of the day is doing what is right in God's eyes, and not the eyes of man.

Notes:

March 16

Your willpower will get you there, but it won't keep you there. Remember why you started, and you'll go the distance every time. Although you may not trust yourself at times, trust in God since He is the one who created you and has given you the dream as well as the wherewithal to achieve it.

While I recognize that I fall short of Your grace, Lord Jesus, I desire to carry out the plan You have for my life. While this path might be difficult and taxing at times, please give me the strength to persevere. AMEN!

Notes:

March 17

Each of us is on a different path, and each of our lives serves a different purpose and vision. As a result, none of us should ever wish for what someone else has. What is intended for you is intended for you. We don't want to undertake anything until we have the necessary resources and mindset. What we seek can sometimes be a curse rather than a blessing. The question we should be asking ourselves is "Why am I pursuing and needing something that is not mine and was not created for me?" Most of the time, the answer is found within ourselves rather than outside of us.

Notes:

March 18

When we are presented with uncomfortable truths about ourselves, it is never easy. It might be downright difficult at times, but owning and changing it is critical. When individuals in your inner circle criticize or reflect on your shortcomings, see it as an opportunity rather than a setback and grab the chance to improve. Those that truly love and care for you will never be afraid to tell you the painful truth.

Notes:

March 19

Never allow someone the authority to make you feel inadequate; if you have, reclaim it. Refuse to accept anything just because it is presented to you. Knowing who you are and where you come from is critical for plotting your future route. Sacrificing one's own self-respect, decency, and authenticity in order to meet the requirements of others and feel at ease in their presence is obsurd. You were made by and for the best. If you remember that, you will never have to play second fiddle or be made to feel less than who you are.

Notes:

March 20

Keeping the grief of the past close to us just makes us feel worse and inhibits us from being the best versions of ourselves. Learning to let go and allowing God to take control is the smartest decision you will ever make in your life. There are some variables that are beyond our control. Attempting to fix the situation on our own risks making it even more complicated than it is. Seek God first in all things, and your steps will be ordered.

Notes:

March 21

We can't continue to blame others and the world for what we can and cannot do in this life. We have not because we ask not. When what God has instilled deep inside your very being consumes your every waking moment, then you will pursue it. If it doesn't consume you, you don't want it bad enough. After all, if it were easy, everyone would do it.

Notes:

March 22

We only have the ability to change ourselves. I don't know about you, but keeping up with my own business is a job in and of itself and takes a lot of my time. The only person we can change is ourselves. It is perplexing why we continuously subject ourselves to the burden trying to assert control over someone else? Real change can only start within ourselves. The environment around us will change if we change how we process information, how we react to it, and how we deal with unproductive thinking.

Notes:

March 23

For every finger you point at others, there will be three pointing back at you. You are three times as guilty as the person you have on trial. God has granted us all grace for the wrong we have done in the past as well as the wrong we are doing now and in the future. Therefore, we should afford others the same. No one is perfect. Judge not unless you be judged.

Dear Jesus, I sometimes open my mouth before determining whether or not what I have to say is beneficial. When I speak to or about others, I don't want to come out as arrogant or critical. Create a clean heart in me, Oh Lord, so that I can recognize the good rather than the faults of others. AMEN!

Notes:

March 24

In order to give 100% of ourselves, we have to be healthy. It is a must, not a choice. When we are unhealthy, we are not operating at full capacity. Give yourself the opportunity to be great at whatever it is you set out to do. Our health is so important to our everyday lives and those around us, especially family and friends, and people we have yet to meet. Get out of your own way, get the help you need, pick yourself up, and be grrrrrreeeeeeat!

Only you, Lord Jesus, can see what the naked eye cannot, and you alone know what lurks under the surface. Help me to take better care of myself so that I can live fully to complete all of the tasks I've been assigned. AMEN!

Notes:

March 25

Our faith was spawned from something we feared. We were all afraid of something at some point in time, but we did it anyway, which developed our faith. Don't be fearful of stepping out and being your authentic self, meeting people you've never met, or doing something you've never done. Do not be afraid to not to do anything. There are people out there waiting to meet you and to receive what you have to offer. You will never reach them if you are too afraid to try.

Notes:

March 26

Typically, when we grow and change, we do it alone. We can't expect for the world to change just because we did. Oftentimes, we get frustrated with others because they aren't where we are. But that is ok; it just means that you are growing and outgrowing people. It is still ok to love them, but you have to make the decision: "Am I getting what I need at this stage of my journey?" or, "Do I need to seek people that will help advance me to the next level?" Don't get me wrong! I am not saying that you need to throw people away. However, seek out people that will help you get to the next level, and can assist you in this phase of your journey. It will require new focus, new mindset, and new people.

Notes:

March 27

There is a reason for the season that you are in. Nothing is wasted. The hard times are there to give us strength, grow us, and guide us in the direction where our destiny resides. That heartache we once felt should have taught us a lesson in love. That disrespect that was so generously given to us should have taught us respect for others. That difficult person in our lives should have taught us about different personalities and proved to us that we are stronger than we know. Nothing will break you if you learn the lesson in each trial.

Notes:

March 28

There are some people in your life that mean you no good. Just as there are people there to get you to the next level, there are also people there to keep you stagnant. Pay attention to your circle of people. Keep who needs to be kept and purge who needs to be purged. It is ok to loose someone to save yourself.

Jesus, Lord, I wasn't always a good judge of char-acter. So much so that the same people you tried to separate from me, I drew back into my life. Help me make better decisions. AMEN!

Notes:

March 29

When you know who you are, you will refuse to be treated anything less than that. Your purpose on this earth is not to be treated less than a human being. Your purpose is divine, tailored by God, and full of His blessings. It is time you address the elephant in the room and call it what it is. "This relationship is toxic, and I deserve better." Do what needs to be done and make the decision.

Lord Jesus, sometimes I go along to get along. I've let others persuade me to do things I wouldn't typically do. I said things I wouldn't typically say and in ways I wouldn't normally speak. Please help me to stay firm on what is right and wrong. AMEN!

Notes:

March 30

There will be closed doors only God can open and open doors only He can close. It is imperative that you recognize when God's hand is at work. We pray and pray and ask him for things, and when He answers, we don't even recognize what it is. You must remember that God is not like man. Everything He does, He does exceedingly and abundantly above and beyond anything we can think of or imagine. Therefore, whatever it is you are asking for, pray that He gives you eyes to see and ears to hear so that you recognize it is Him and not dismiss it as we tend to do because it isn't wrapped in the packaging we expect it to be.

Notes:

March 31

Anything worth having is worth waiting for. We must learn to be patient in all things. Ask yourself, "Am I even prepared to receive it?" Oftentimes, we are not. If you are expecting something major in your life, you must prepare for it. If it is a purchase, you will save money; if it is a house, you will draw up plans. Whate-ver it is, you prepare. Rushing it and being impatient can introduce imperfections and less than quality results. Be patient.

Notes:

April 1

Our trials are like climbing a mountain. Each adversity takes us closer and closer to our destination. Adversity doesn't necessarily mean we did anything wrong. Sometimes, God uses people, places, and things to move us along. Just think about it; once we make it to the top of the mountain, we will be able to rejoice and thank God that although it was a rough journey, He never left our side. He was with us every step of the way.

Notes:

April 2

As much as we would love to have our families stand behind us no matter what, that is not always the case. Regardless of the situation, not everyone will always be happy about your growth. There may be times our growth appears to make people feel a certain way. "You've changed" is the most common phrase I have heard. We try arguing the fact that we are the same people we have always been, but that couldn't be further from the truth. Where there is growth, there must be change. You simply cannot have one without the other. The next time someone says to you, "You've changed," reply by saying, "Yes, I did."

Notes:

April 3

Get in alignment with the things you desire. You cannot pray for things and be ill-prepared to receive them because they can and will slip through your fingers. No matter how big or small the desire, preparation is key to attaining and keeping that which you seek.

Jesus, Lord, I want to be ready when my prayers are answered. Build me up to be ready. I don't want to pass up the opportunity You're providing for me. I want to and need to be prepared. AMEN!

Notes:

April 4

It is true that our judgment is imperfect. We can't always trust ourselves or our decisions. Let's face it, we have all made some bad decisions in our lives. As a result, we must put our trust in the one who created us. The one who knows what's best for us. The one who knows us better than ourselves. It is a must that we have faith in God, even a tiny morsel of it will do. There was a plan and a purpose placed deep within us when we were developed in our mother's womb. Nothing on earth will or can stop us from our God given destiny. Can it be postponed, yes. Can it be deterred, absolutely. But never, will it ever be denied.

Notes:

April 5

Having faith is our greatest possession. Yes, our journey can sometimes seem bleak, but our faith is what keeps us pressing forward. It's easy to become afraid of things that we don't know the outcome of, or when we add our own ending to the story. When you run out of options, trust in your Creator. Debilitating fear is not in God's plan for us. Fear does not come from the Lord.

Help me, Lord Jesus, to trust and believe in what I cannot see or feel. I try my hardest to hold on to your words, but Lord, it's difficult at times to believe in what you cannot see. I really want to believe. Please, Lord, grant me faith. AMEN!

Notes:

April 6

Negative behavior begets negative behavior. When we are at a loss, feeling hurt, dejected or angry, combating those feelings with alcohol, drugs, promiscuity, etc., is a dead-end road. It will definitely numb the pain momentarily, but sooner or later, reality comes seeking its moment. This is the reason addiction is prevalent in the lives of millions. The more you consume, the more you begin to build a tolerance for what you crave. What used to take only a little bit of this or that now has evolved into an enormous beast that can no longer be tamed. Don't be afraid to seek help when life spirals out of control. Be afraid NOT to get the help you need. Truth is, if you could have fixed the problem on your own, no problem would exist.

Notes:

April 7

Have you ever been driving down the street and a little voice told you to "turn here" or "don't turn there," but you did the opposite of what the voice was telling you to do? Or you had a feeling in the pit of your stomach that something was off about the person you were interested in. However, you ignored it? That was the small voice of God ordering your steps. We often ignore this voice and, instead, choose to do our own thing. This is why difficult times are present in our lives: because we don't listen to that small voice. If we would just get out of our own way and adhere to His voice, we would save ourselves a tremendous amount of heartache and grief.

Notes:

April 8

For the majority of the human population, things just don't fall into our laps. Most of us were not born with a silver spoon in our mouths. We have had to work for everything that we want in life. Sitting back wishing for a job never got anyone hired. Praying is the best thing any of us can do for anything we want to acquire in this life. However, prayer without action is ineffective. It is the same analogy. Praying for something you are not willing to do your part in is also ineffective. Truth be told, we tend to appreciate things more when we work for them instead of them being handed to us.

Notes:

April 9

Have you ever missed out on something because you were not prepared for it? Well, let me tell you, I have. It's downright sad that something you have been praying and wishing for is within your grasp, but because you are ill-prepared, you are not able to take advantage of the opportunity. One of the most difficult things you could ever witness is seeing your "blessing" utilized by someone else, and there is not a thing you can do about it. Get into place! Get ready to be ready!

Notes:

April 10

Not going after our dreams and aspirations is no one's fault but our own. We are never too old to live the life God has planned for us. Blaming others is scapegoating. When we were children, we blame our parents and other outside sources for things not happening for us. But as an adult, your future is in your hands. I was 47 years old when I went back to school and 50 when I got my first degree. We must stop blaming others and make things happen for ourselves. Anything else is just an excuse.

Notes:

April 11

There is a reason for the season you are currently experiencing. No experience, no matter how pleasant, bad, or indifferent, is ever discarded. Even if it is unpleasant and painful at times. The process will teach you key lessons that are critical for your growth and recovery along your journey.

Lord Jesus,I recognize that both good and bad times will come. The truth is that I need help getting through both. Left alone with the good times I may destroy myself. Left alone with the bad times it will destroy me. Never leave me Lord, I can't do anything without you. AMEN!

Notes:

April 12

There are no coincidences for Christ-followers. There is a reason and a purpose for everything. If you lose your job, it means that there is a better one waiting for you, or that job is keeping you from God and your destiny. A relationship ends, their season ends, and the purge begins. Whatever it is, whether good, terrible, or indifferent, it serves a purpose. Be of good courage; wait on the Lord, as the Bible instructs: "Be strong, and let your heart take courage, all you who wait for the Lord!" (ESV Psalm 31:24)

Notes:

April 13

Don't allow others to tell you who you are or how you should behave. You are meant for greatness; all you need to do is believe in yourself. It doesn't matter what other people say or think. What is important is what the Master has to say. People have found it necessary to disparage one another since the beginning of time. What gives us the right to assume that we are so unique that this will never happen to us? Just keep your mind on God and not on other people, and He will provide whatever you need at precisely the appropriate time.

Notes:

April 14

Whether you believe it or not, you have a mission in life that you must complete. Your assignment is the driving force behind your existence. There are several plans already in place and ready for your use. You must conceive it in order to achieve it.

Thank you, Lord, for the gift of life today. I thank you for every gift, vision, and desire. Assist me in becoming the person you created me to be. When I am weak, be my strength. AMEN!

Notes:

April 15

As someone that loves and adores her family, I am a firm believer in showing them how much they mean to me. No one should ever have to guess our love for them. The worst thing to ever happen is to lose a loved one, having never shown them how appreciated they were during their life. We cannot bring loved ones back after they're gone, but we can definitely love them while they are around to enjoy it. Make sure to give them their roses today.

Notes:

April 16

Every day we are given the chance to open our eyes is a good day! It is a blessing to be able to get out of bed and dress ourselves in the morning. There are people out there praying to be in our shoes that they had the one or two things we complain about. We must be cautious about what we whine or complain about because life can change on a dime. Maintain a grateful attitude today and everyday.

Lord, teach me to be grateful to others. I don't want to be seen as taking others for granted. It matters how we treat others, and I want to be kind to both those I know and those I don't.

Notes:

April 17

It's not always about crossing the finish line, but about enjoying the scenery along the way. Sometimes we get so caught up in life, focusing on our objective, that we overlook the joys, lessons, and growth we had along the way. It's the same as eating so quickly that you don't relish the taste, texture, or flavor of your food. Take it easy! There is always beauty to be discovered. Enjoy the flavor!

Lord, I want to go through this life learning and embracing all that it entails. Help me to slow down, embrace my moments, and smell the roses along the way. AMEN!

Notes:

April 18

Just because you were mistreated in a relationship doesn't mean the next person that comes along will have that same behavior. Learning to let go of old hurts will allow you to embrace new relationships. Oftentimes, we tend to make people in our life suffer because of past relationships, by not giving the new one a chance because we fear getting hurt again. If we are going to try a new relationship, we need a new mindset. We have to be willing to be vulnerable. The truth is that everyone is different, and the only way to get to your happy place is to step out and try again. Never give up on life. Never give up on love. If someone is not living up to your standard of treatment for yourself, let them go and move on. For every one that won't, there will be another one that will.

Notes:

April 19

Learning to accept who you are and the person God created you to be is one of the greatest tasks you will ever accomplish. We can be our own worst enemy sometimes, comparing ourselves to others. We wished we looked like this or talked like that, not realizing that, that is a sin in and of itself. You were created perfectly, flaws and all. Learn to embrace the person you are 100%: every scar, curve, and wrinkle. What you see as imperfect is God's masterpiece. You were created for the best by the best. As soon as you face that reality, you will no longer worry about what you are not but will bask in everything that you are.

Notes:

April 20

When the one you love is not loving you back, you must let it go. We are enough, just as we are. We do not need validation from irrelevant external sources. If you allow others to treat you any type of way they will. It is up to you to set a standard for your life, because if you don't, someone else will.

Jesus, Lord, I don't want to be a pawn in someone else's deranged fantasy. Assist me in standing in the truth of who I am in You. Give me the strength to abandon harmful habits and those who do not honor or respect me. I know who You are; all I need to do now is remember who I am in You. AMEN!

Notes:

April 21

True friendships are not about others continuously agreeing with our actions and behaviors. It is about those that are brave enough to call us out when we are wrong and when we need someone to be open and honest with us. Anyone in your life that is just there to get along is not who you need in your circle. True friends care about what you care about and help you become the person you are destined to be.

Notes:

April 22

We have all done some things that have caused shame and regret in our lives. We can either use that mistake as an excuse to remain stagnant where we are, or we can use it as a teachable moment, which will thrust you into our future. Turn that shame and regret into power and feel the freedom that it brings into your life.

Jesus, I know that you have forgiven me of all the wrong I have done. I need some help in forgiving myself. I am constantly rehashing the past, I want to free myself from self defeating thoughts. Help me Lord. AMEN!

Notes:

April 23

Discover what you love, and I promise you will love what you do. It's not an easy task to be afforded an opportunity to say we absolutely love what we do for a living. If every day you wake up with regret about going to a specific job, place, or event, perhaps it is time for you to do something different. Pray on it, seek counsel, but most importantly, do not be afraid to let go and find what you love.

Notes:

April 24

Denying oneself of anything we crave is not only good for the flesh but also for the spirit. Another term used for denying the flesh is called fasting. If you ever want to strengthen in the spirit, deny the flesh of the thing it craves. Fasting is a promise between you and God. Some people fast with food, social media, sweets, or anything the body craves. Deny yourself whatever that temptation is and press on and watch what God will do.

Notes:

April 25

We can become very complacent with our lives, so much to the point that we miss out on grand opportunities because we don't like to change. We will never discover all the wonderful things the Lord has for us by settling. Laziness is not of God. The enemy comes to kill, steal, and destroy, and the last thing he wants is for us to reach our full potential. So, embrace change. The possibilities for your life are endless, with God in your corner.

Notes:

April 26

We have all been through some tough times in our lives, but we made it to the other side. The lessons we have learned from our trials and tribulations will someday bless someone else. There is someone out there seeking our voice, our story. They need to see someone who has come through the very thing they are going through now. God has pulled you through that situation to show you no matter what happens in life; He has you covered. Our job is to show the world how good our God is. We can only do that through our testimony of what He has brought us through.

Notes:

April 27

There is someone out there thinking they are not going to survive the challenge they are currently going through. They need to know that they can and will make it through if they hold on and just believe. We can never see our way out when we are consumed with grief and worry. However, God always provides. He doesn't wake up one day thinking, "I am not going to help this person or that person today." He is the God of grace and mercy. He will send us a helpline because He is never-changing.

Notes:

April 28

We have all heard it said, "Find the thing that gives you meaning, and joy and money will be a bonus," Actually, it is true. You won't have to work a day in your life if you do what you love. Of course, it's much simpler to say than to actually accomplish. But making the effort to figure it out is worthwhile. Put your trust in yourself. Take a chance on yourself. Explore opportunities that have been brought to you or that you seek, and let's see what's possible!

Notes:

April 29

Don't allow other people's bad behavior to con-taminate the person you are. We are guilty by asso-ciation, which is sometimes the worst accusation there is. Being blamed for others' actions is like being incarcerated for a crime you did not commit. Wise up and protect yourself. "If any of you lacks wisdom, let him ask God, who gives generously to all without reproach, and it will be given him" (James 1:5 ESV).

Notes:

April 30

When I was a little girl, I was envious of my friends for one reason or another. Some prettier, some athletic, some singers, some socially inclined, and most had good relationships with their parents. I would always find something in them that I wished I had. It wasn't until later in life that I learned what was for me was for me. Every mole, every scar, and even the slant in my eyes was the very thing that made me stand out. We are all uniquely created by the Master crafter. Everything about us is intentional because God does not make mistakes.

Notes:

May 1

Nothing is more powerful than a transformed men-tality, whether good, negative, or indifferent. When we alter our opinions about something, our world shifts to accommodate us. All we need to do if we want something different in and out of life is change our minds. Align yourself with the right people, places, and things to help us get what we need to succeed.

Notes:

May 2

No two journeys are the same, similar perhaps, but never the same. We don't have the grace to run someone else's race. Understanding your path in life is key to your journey. What appears as a blessing for others can be a curse for those not fully equipped. That is why the Bible instructs us not to covet our neighbor's house. Enjoy your journey. It was tailor-made just for you.

Notes:

May 3

Don't allow the actions and attitudes of others to alter your course. There have been times I was so angry at people that I did not operate in my full capacity because I gave my power away. Allowing people to dictate your mood gives them complete and full control over your life. The result is never favorable but the opposite of everything you know and believe in yourself. It will turn you into someone and something you are not.

Notes:

May 4

There may be times your good and kind gestures may go unnoticed and even unappreciated. Do it regardless. Not because of who they are, but because of who you are. We must always take the high road because that is where our blessing lies. The way you leave people will forever be imprinted on their hearts and minds.

Lord, help me not be so focused on man but totally on you. People will let me down, but you Lord, you never have and you never will. Lord, help me to stand strong in all that I do and all that I am. AMEN!

Notes:

May 5

There are many kinds of adversity, and not all are intended to kill you. There are times when you need obstacles in your path to propel you forward, advance you to the next level, and clear the way. When you have triumphed over adversity, you will not be the person you were before. You will emerge from this experience more robust and wiser. Our most essential and indispensable instructor is life itself, and it cannot be avoided.

Notes:

May 6

It's not about what happened to us; in fact, we are who we are because of those things. Yes, it was most certainly unpleasant and even painful. However, we emerged from the flames, bruised but not destroyed. That is the wonderful thing about God. He has a way of using those things meant to destroy us to help us progress.

Lord, I know you have a mighty plan for my life. The only reason I am here today is of because of it. I ask that just as you have always been by my side and carried me through the storms of my life, that you continue doing so. I thank you in advance. AMEN!

Notes:

May 7

Change what you think about (and speak about), and your outlook on life will change with it. Change always starts in our minds. If we are not willing to change what we think about on a daily basis, we will never become what we dream of becoming. Change your mind and the ways you speak to yourself, and everything changes.

Lord Jesus, I don't want to destroy my life with negative and unimpactful words. I want to flourish in all that I do and say. Quicken my spirit at the sign of self destruction oh Lord. AMEN

Notes:

May 8

We are blessed not because of who we are but because of who God is. We all fall short of the goodness and grace of God. He constantly avails to us much more than we deserve. We should never think that we are deserving or worthy of His blessings to the point that we become arrogant and prideful. It is not about who we are but who God is.

Lord God, help me recognize the grace and mercy that only you can bestow upon me. I will not take credit for your actions as my own. Give me a spirit of humility in Jesus name. AMEN

Notes:

May 9

Up to this point in your life, it could have been sealed and riddled with pain and sorrow, grief and anguish, but nevertheless, you are right where you're supposed to be now. Just take a moment to start where you are right now and ask Jesus to help you to fulfill your plan and your purpose for your life in this world. Believe it or not, the greater the struggle, the greater the reward. Just look at Jesus and all He had to endure to save us. Just look at His life and look at all He went through. Look at every cross He had to bear, every whip, tear, and bloodshed He had to endure. But, in the end, He received the ultimate reward, and so did you.

Notes:

May 10

Status and accolades are all given by man, but self-worth comes from the Lord. Once we know who we are and whose we are, our self-worth kicks into action. Validation is then instilled within us, and we no longer need outside sources of confirmation to validate our worth. It's never about what you have; it's always about who you have, and that is Jesus. If we can remember this one thing, we will all be better off.

Notes:

May 11

Have you ever felt like the more you do the right thing, the more trouble comes? Of course, you have! We all have! But never get weary of doing the right thing. When we keep our eyes on God, we don't spend as much time worrying about what the next person has and what we don't have. It's not about anyone, but if you keep your eyes on God, you will stay focused.

Notes:

May 12

Our choices not only affect us, but it affects those around us. We have to decide if we're going to continue to do what's right or if we're going to continue to do what's wrong and suffer the consequences either way. We tend to make better, more informed decisions when we think about others and less about ourselves and what we want. We must say to ourselves: "If I do this, who could it potentially affect? Will the effect be negative or positive?" This will determine what you do and how you do it.

Notes:

May 13

Time is the most precious thing in this world. When you have run out of it, there's no more. When we spend our time on things that do not matter, we take away the opportunity to do something positive for ourselves and others. Every opportunity we do not take advantage of, we will lose.

Lord, please grant me the opportunity to be a blessing in someone else's life. Give me the awareness to be attentive to and perceptive of other people's needs. AMEN!

Notes:

May 14

Start speaking life over your circumstances and over your future today. There's power in our words and in what we say more so than what we do. If you want a life full of joy, peace, honor, and fulfillment, you have to speak it. We have more control than we think we do. If you want to be happy, claim your happiness. If you want to be healthy, claim it. If you want joy in your life, claim it.

Notes:

May 15

Contrary to what you may think or believe, we cannot change what we do not acknowledge. The only way to make a difference in your life today is to change your mind. It all starts with our thought processes. If you don't change your mind, the body will not and cannot follow. A changed mind places the body on notice and will adhere to those changes.

Notes:

May 16

Always give everything you've got to whatever it is you're trying to achieve or do, and do it with as much enthusiasm as possible. When we approach anything with less than our absolute commitment, the quality of the work we produce suffers. But if we give something our all, there is nothing more we can do, and we can declare with complete candor that we gave it our best shot.

Notes:

May 17

Friends are people that we choose to have in our lives. Your family is the people God has chosen to be in our lives. You're in the family you are in because God has given us grace for the people that love us and vice versa. The only reason you can tolerate unpleasantness from them is because of the grace you've been given for them. Love your family, you need them and they need you.

Notes:

May 18

God has a plan for each and every one of us. Never think you do not have a purpose in life because nothing could be further from the truth. We are all created with a master plan in mind. If you are ever unsure and want to find out God's plan for your life, just ask Him to show you.

Lord Jesus, I've heard you have a plan for my life, but to be completely honest with you, Lord, it seems relatively hopeless from where I'm standing. Please let me see my life from your perspective. I need to feel needed, wanted and valued, but I'm not there yet, Lord. Please help me to make the changes I can and let go of the things I can't. AMEN!

Notes:

May 19

Like it or not, I am my sister's and my brother's keeper. We are responsible for one another. We weren't intended to be alone. Even the animals travel together. Since God said we as human beings have dominion over the entire earth, that makes us vastly more important than animals. Take care of one another. Love one another. Have compassion for one another. Honor one another. Protect one another. Rejoice with one another.

Notes:

May 20

Not accepting help when you need it is preposterous! Until a person shows you that they don't have your back, trust that they will. Ultimately, people have your best interest at heart, and they want to see you move forward. There are more people for you than against you.

Lord, help me to understand that you have put individuals in my life for a reason. Let me not be an impediment to my own development. Help me to accept the olive branch they give. Remove any pride that is buried in my heart so that I can allow those who will help me to do so. I am aware that I can get in my own way at times. I need to adjust my thinking right now. Lord, give me strength. AMEN!

Notes:

May 21

Mistakes are not the end all to be all. They are learning tools to help us grow. They are stepping stones to lift us higher than before the mistake. They are developing mechanisms that will help us become better human beings. What they are not are hindrances to keep us stagnant and from moving forward. If it weren't for our failures and mistakes, we wouldn't be who we are today. Just think about it; when we were children learning to walk, had we not failed repeatedly, we wouldn't be walking today. It's only because we got up again when we fell.

Notes:

May 22

Wisdom and intelligence are not the same thing. Wisdom is the peace of God speaking to, leading, and directing you. Being smart simply means being able to outmaneuver others in different situations. Wisdom comes from God, and intelligence can be acquired practically anyplace (school, street corner, friends, literally anywhere someone knows something you do not). If you want wisdom, seek God. If you want to be smart, go to school.

Notes:

May 23

One of my all-time favorite songs in the world is by the King of Pop, Michael Jackson, "The Man in the Mirror." Oh, my Lord! I love that song: "there is no message that could've been any clearer. If you want to make the world a better place, [we] have to take a look at yourself and make that change." Those words are forever etched in my mind, heart and soul. Before we start pointing fingers, laughing at, criticizing, and gossiping about others, we must first inventory the person gazing back at us in the mirror.

Notes:

May 24

It is not about what the world says but what we allow to enter our hearts and spirits. Who are you listening to? Who's voice matters in your life? Are those with the loudest voice relevant, or just loud? If you don't know who you are people will mold you into who and what they want to be? Who, are you paying attention to? Whose opinion counts in your life? Without this vital information, we are puppets. "Whoever dwells in the shadow of the Almighty will rest in the shelter of the Most High" (Psalms 91:1 NIV).

Notes:

May 25

We are the most important component of the plan that God has devised. You're not a mistake or a coincidence. You are an integral part of the wheel of life, you must play the hand you have been dealt. Nobody else on this entire planet is capable of playing your role as well as you can. No one else even comes close. Accept the place that is rightfully yours and make the most of the time you have left.

Notes:

May 26

In a world with billions of people, we may feel like we are the only person. You are not alone. Our God is always ready, willing, and able to step in and take the burden for you. You can always count on him to be there for you. You only need to make the request, that when He brings you to something that He will also lead you through it.

This is such a terrible and lonely world, Lord Jesus. Send us someone to console us in our loneliness. We are never alone with or in you. Give us courage for what is to come. In Jesus' name. AMEN!

Notes:

May 27

God doesn't make mistakes. Everything you need to do has been instilled inside your being. You are enough, you are adequate, and you are resilient. You, yes, you, can do any and all things through Christ, which strengthens you. So, lift your chin up. Be of good courage. You've got this!

Nothing happens under or over the sun that you are not aware of, Lord Jesus. I'm not sure what my strengths or talents are. Please, Lord, bring them to the forefront of my consciousness so that I can operate in them. I thank you, Lord, for being you. AMEN!

Notes:

May 28

If you want to forget about your problems and your issues, show a little kindness to someone else. There's no better way to forget about what we're going through than to extend a loving arm to someone in need. When we focus on others and not ourselves, we tend to forget about ourselves. So, show others kindness today. All is well.

Notes:

May 29

God did not create us to worry. Worrying is for those that do not know the Lord. To worry is to say, I don't trust you, Lord. When we worry, we do not trust that God is who He says He is. That God cannot do what He says He will do. Worrying is contradictory to our faith. Trust in the Lord. Lean on Him. Worry and faith cannot occupy the same space, so choose wisely.

Notes:

May 30

If God wanted you to be like Mary down the street, He would have created you as Mary. The reason why God made you the way He did is that the universe needed what you have. Wishing that we were someone we're not is a slap in the face to God. We never know what others go through to attain and maintain what they have. We must learn to be comfortable in our own skin and with what we have now. We are where we are supposed to be now and who we are supposed to be.

Notes:

May 31

Being nasty and cruel requires additional effort. It is work, hard work at that. The practice of compassion requires the least amount of effort. If I choose kindness rather than cruelty, it may be possible to save another person's life. When someone is suffering or going through challenges in their lives, we never know how effective a kind word could be. It could mean the difference between life and death. Pay attention to the things you say to other people. Choose wisely.

Notes:

June 1

Challenges are an inconvenience, but they must be endured to play the game of life. It's possible that they are not what we desire for our life. Looking back, we realize that our challenges have been vital to our growth. Not only have they taught us valuable lessons, but they also brought us closer to God. They have helped us become the people He needed us to be and planted us in the places He wanted us to be.

Notes:

June 2

Have you ever had someone heavenly on your mind and later found out they were ill, hurt, or passed away. You beat yourself up for not calling or going to see about them when you had the chance. This is one of the worst feelings to experience. It is a nudge that something is wrong. Something is off with them. It can also be an implication to pray for that person. It is always good to pray for someone weighing heavily on our hearts. It is a nudging of the spirit for us to intercede on behalf of that person. We put things off for another day, another time, assuming there will be one. The next thing we know, the opportunity is no longer available, and regret sets in. Don't let that happen. Act on those subtle nudges from God. Do it now, for tomorrow is not promised to any of us.

Notes:

June 3

You are important. Without you, the world would be void of your precious gift. We cannot adequately care for other people if we're not OK. Water does not flow from an empty basin. Take care of yourself today. Take that medicine like you should, drink plenty of water, and see a therapist. Do what you have to do to take care of yourself. You are important.

Lord Jesus help me to see the value I add to this world and to those you have placed in my charge. Help me to take better care of myself so that I can take better care of others. AMEN!

Notes:

June 4

The Lord will always give us an out for any situation we may encounter. There will be an escape route to prevent us from making bad and life-altering decisions if we are willing to listen to His still, small voice. The same voice that tells us to make a right when we want to go left. The same voice that whispers run when we want to stay. There is always an option with God.

Lord Jesus, I don't always follow your voice and guidance, and have often suffered considerably. I no longer wish to go on my own accord or to respond to my desires. Lord, I want and need instruction from you. AMEN!

Notes:

June 5

If you can conceive it, you can achieve it! Those out-of-this-world ideas, visions, and aspirations you've had come from God, not you. Therefore, it's attainable! So, don't talk yourself out of it. After all, it's not about you. It's about fulfilling the assignment God has placed on you for this world.

Lord, I have hopes and dreams for myself and my family, but you have plans that are bigger than my mind could ever comprehend. Teach me to slow down and wait on you Lord. AMEN!

Notes:

June 6

Learn to love yourself. You are just as significant as the people you love. Sometimes, the love for ourselves gets lost in the shuffle and we play second fiddle to others. But this is not how it should be. We should always treat others the way we would like to be treated, this includes ourselves. We should be confident enough to know we are not less than anyone.

Lord, allow me to see how important I am. I sometimes feel like I'm always at the bottom and not enough. I want to be okay with who and what I am rather than focusing on who I am not. AMEN!

Notes:

June 7

Everyone in our lives has a vital role to perform. Some folks who begin with us will not and cannot always finish with us. We grow, and in the process, we sometimes outgrow people. It does not imply that you do not care about them. It does not mean that you dislike them. It indicates that you are changing and moving into a season of your life and cannot take them with you. Love should not be based on whether you remain stationary or go forward.

Notes:

June 8

There are numerous ways to be kind to someone. Sometimes all that is required is a sympathetic ear or a shoulder to cry on. It is not always necessary for us to give our input, offer advice, or even help them. Sometimes all they need to know is that you're willing to listen to what they say.

Lord, show me your ways, so I can be kind to those I contact regularly. I want to make a positive impact in the lives of others, not just myself. Lord, today I release this, my heart's yearning to you. AMEN!

Notes:

June 9

At every opportunity, inspire someone. We all need a little encouragement from time to time, and if it wasn't for someone encouraging us in our weakest moments, we might not be where we are today or who we are. Our primary existence is to help one another, not ourselves. Our refusal to do just that is never an option.

Lord, make me impactful to the lives of those around me. Help me to know when to push, when to pull and when to let go. Thank you in advance, Lord. AMEN!

Notes:

June 10

Because of your contagious optimism and attitude, some individuals will take a chance on you even if you lack qualifications. This is because of your positive attitude and personality. It is not always about what you know; it is sometimes the opposite of what you would expect. Always allow the real and authentic you to show up at all times.

Lord, I want to have faith in the person you made me to be. I don't want to act like someone I'm not. Teach me to love myself as much as you do. In areas where I lack confidence, breathe in my direction so that I do not stumble and become a victim.

Notes:

June 11

Every time we wish a day was other than the day it is, we are wishing our lives away. Next time you say to yourself, "I wish today was Friday," don't say it out loud. Once you put it into the atmosphere, it becomes activated. Learn to embrace every moment of every day. Think of it this way. Because Friday is closest to Monday (not the other way around), it will come quicker than you make like, so be careful. Time will not slow down just for the weekend and speed up on the weekday. Be carfeul of what you wish for, because sometimes those wishes do come true.

Notes:

June 12

Each and every person created has hopes, dreams, and desires. We must always ask that our wants to stay in line with God's plan. This will ensure the very best outcome. There have been times in my life when I wanted my will and not God's, and as a result, I suffered from the consequences of those actions. Stay in God's will. Pray on it and be encouraged.

Lord Jesus, there are some thngs that I desire for myself and my family, but I always want it to be in your will not mine. If it is in your will and your plan, let it be done, If it is not, remove it from my heart so that I may move forward. AMEN!

Notes:

June 13

My Bible says in Proverbs 29:13: "Where there is no vision, people perish." The vision we have for our lives is a glimpse into the future. What we see in those visions is attainable if we keep the dream and vision killers at bay. So, keep your eyes on God and stay committed to where he is taking you. Trust and believe that God will guide you each every step of the way.

Notes:

June 14

We all have something to say. We should no longer be silent, nor should we be quiet, because the world is waiting for our input. Our voice is not just a noisemaker; it's a mechanism of change. Use your voice to help make a positive change in this world, and use it wisely. Be productive instead of provocative. Your words represent you more than anything as it embodies your thoughts.

Notes:

June 15

Trying to do something we've never done before can be intimidating and downright scary. Let that be the fuel that propels us into our future, not hold us back. It's natural to be afraid, but don't let it paralyze you. Use it as a defense mechanism, not as a source of defeat.

Lord, there are times when I am afraid of the unknown. I want to be fearless in both my gifts and my journey. Despite my fears, please assist me in moving forward. When I can't see what's in front of me, I want to trust you. I want to see you when I can't see any other way. AMEN!

Notes:

June 16

Being stagnant and afraid to take chances is no way to have a fulfilled life. Life has a way of evolving, with us unaware of what will happen next. Although we may not always have the answers, we must keep moving forward, asking for help throughout the journey and trusting that God always has a better plan for us.

I want to be productive with the things I need to do, but Lord, sometimes I find it hard to get going. I don't want to miss out on opportunites because of laziness and complacency. Lord teach me how to move forward when my mind and body want to do the opposite.

Notes:

June 17

As adults, we must take responsibility for ourselves. What happened to us as children can no longer be the excuse for bad behavior as adults. Once we become responsible for our own lives, we are also accountable for our actions and their consequences, and therefore, our fate as well.

Jesus, I don't always want to accept responsibility for what I say and do, but I understand that failing to do so will not benefit, but hinder my life. I want to be unwavering, trustworthy, and honest. AMEN!

Notes:

June 18

Always assume those we encounter are important and deserve respect. We never know if the people we help or don't help are angels disguised as people testing our intentions and deeds. "Don't forget to show hospitality to strangers, for some who have done this have entertained angels without realizing it!" (He-brews 13:2 NLT).

Notes:

June 19

Looking for your purpose? Matthew 7:7 states: "Ask, and it will be given to you; seek, and you will find; knock, and the door will be opened to you." You have a purpose. Pray for it to be shown to you and then proceed accordingly. Look for the signs that God gives you in your life, and pay heed to them. If you wish for God to guide you, you must give your heart fully to Him.

Notes:

June 20

We must learn to be strong and stop answering to what others have called us. First of all, you are the daughter or son of the King, and people don't have authority over you. Only God does. Regardless of what people say or think about you, don't be moved by it. You just focus on being the best version of yourself that you can possibly be.

Notes:

June 21

Change what is in your power to change. Pray about that which cannot change. Stressing about cir-cumstances out of your control is like saying God can't fix it, or that He will not see you through it. Recite the Serenity Prayer if you need more enco-uragement, it was written for times such as this: "God grant me the serenity to accept the things I cannot change, courage to change the things I can, and the wisdom to know the difference."

Notes:

June 22

Holding onto the past hinders your journey into the future. When life answers the call for new and better, be sure you are not the one standing in your own way. Let go and explore the possibilities. Your past does not have to define you anymore. Holding onto it only means you are keeping yourself from the endless possibilities that may come to you.

Notes:

June 23

As long as we live and breathe, there will be some things that are going to take the wind from our sails. There will also be disappointments, hurts, bruises, and sorrows. But with all of that, we still possess the power to become a victim or a victor. Change what you can change, but for that in which you cannot, ask your heavenly Father for strength and guidance, and He will guide you to the people who can and will help you maneuver through it.

Notes:

June 24

When you're about to give up and throw in the towel, that's when you push through and make it to the other side. It's time to break free from whatever has been holding you back. Hold on tight! Your problem's solution is on its way. Don't take the cowards way out. God only helps those who help themselves.

Notes:

June 25

When we do not treat ourselves like the diamonds we are, we cheat ourselves out of the love and kindness we so graciously provide for others daily. Why do we think everyone deserves good things to happen for them, but when it comes to ourselves, we don't think so? Today, I implore you to treat yourself as a priority number one because you are.

Notes:

June 26

To look at someone side-eyed because you don't feel they meet your expectations says more about us than the person you are criticizing. Get your nose out of the air and stop thinking you are the kit and caboodle because you are not. We must treat everyone we encounter the same way we would want them to treat ourselves.

Notes:

June 27

Constructive criticism is valuable for every aspect of our lives. Without it, we have the potential for more mistakes. If someone offers you constructive criticism, humbly accept it; if it is not meant to help you believe me, you will recognize its malice.

Lord give me ears to hear and a heart to accecpt constructive criticism. I need and want to grow through what I go through. Amen!

Notes:

June 28

Have you ever heard, "A rushed job never gets done"? Well, it doesn't. It makes a mess that has to be cleaned up over and over again. Time is of the essence. Relish, embrace, and savor the moment. If you are going to invest the time to do something, at the very least, do your best and get the job done.

Notes:

June 29

When you wake up each morning, what is the first thing you do? Each day we wake up is a new chance, new opportunity; it's all new. What are the things you say when you first awake in the morning? Do you take just a moment to say thank you God? If you do not, let this be the last day you do not acknowledge God before you begin your day. It sets the tone for your entire day.

Notes:

June 30

There is absolutely nothing wrong with needing help and asking for help. People have strategically been positioned in your life for a reason. Pride has never gotten anyone anywhere. Reach out and ask for help when you need it. Asking for help is a gift to the giver, and a blessing for the receiver. Don't deny yourself the blessing.

Notes:

July 1

How can you expect someone else to treat you like a queen when you treat yourself like a pauper ? People are watching and taking notes on how you treat YOURSELF. Rest assured that they will mimic the same behavior You are showing yourself. Therefore, we must be mindful to perform self-care for we are precious cargo.

Notes:

July 2

Never be hard on yourself when you fall because without falling, you never learn to walk. We all make mistakes. Some are worse than others, however, the lessons that we have learned from those mistakes is immeasurable. For each mistake, countless lessons are learned as a result and will benefit us throughout the course of our life.

Notes:

July 3

Haters come in all different genders, races, and religions. They have one job, and that is to cut you off at every turn. Their only loyalty is to your demise. The only good thing they offer is that when they show up, it's a sign you are doing something right. While they are talking, laughing, and criticizing, you are making a difference. You are a change maker. Keep pressing.

Notes:

July 4

Guilty by association is not always black and white. Oftentimes, it's skewed. When people behave badly, it's not our job to right their wrongs. Sometimes, the best and the only thing that we can do is walk away, and rather quickly. People are people and they are going to do and be what and who they are, so just let them do that.

Notes:

July 5

The grace and mercy of God is free to us all. We are here today for no other reason than His grace and mercy. We are not worthy, but He treats us as though we are. The same mercy that has been bestowed upon us, must be graciously passed on to others for the same reason. Not because they deserve it, but because we all fall short.

Notes:

July 6

Why do we say we will do something tomorrow when, in actuality, we have no clue as to what tomorrow will bring, if anything? Why not do what we need to do today and let tomorrow take care of itself? The only time we actually have is right now. Matthew 6:34 states: "Therefore do not worry about tomorrow, for tomorrow will worry about its own things. Sufficient for the day is its own trouble." Enjoy the NOW!

Notes:

July 7

The reason people can't or don't appreciate things they didn't work for is because it didn't cost them anything. When we put our blood sweat, tears, and money into something, we tend to handle it with care. People that do not have respect for money will not manage it wisely. Without having to work for what you have, you are not able to place value on it. Appreciate the things you have worked so hard for.

Notes:

July 8

We have to learn to place the blame where it belongs, which is with ourselves most of the time. 99% of the things we blame others for actually belong to us. It's hard to take a good look at ourselves and address the elephant in the mirror, but it is not only necessary, it's freeing. Own your mistakes and the lessons that come from them.

Notes:

July 9

Were you aware that our children do not belong to us? They belong to God. They have been entrusted to us to lead, and guide them until they reach the age where they can be responsible for themselves. This is why it is a splendid idea to dedicate them back to the Lord when they are born because, truth be told, we don't know what we are doing, we have to lean on the Lord to guide us.

Notes:

July 10

Don't let other peoples negativity suck you down their rabbit hole. Peoples situations calls for us to run as fast as our legs and feet will take us. Negativity is contagious and toxic. It seeks to attach itself to unsuspecting victims, the innocent and the weak. When you feel something tugging on you to leave and or to run, do so with gusto. Sometimes, warning signs only come once, so we must be discerning and ask God for guidance.

Notes:

July 11

What we say to and about others tells the condition of the heart. It is quite possible to speak one thing while doing the opposite. Challenges arise when what we say doesn't line up with what we do. Making a conscious effort to try to do and be better is saying not only to yourself and the world, I can, and I will be the person I need to be.

A good person produces good things from the treasury of a good heart, and an evil person produces evil things from the treasury of an evil heart. Matthew 12:35 (NLT)

Notes:

July 12

Just as there is a silver lining to every dark cloud we have encountered throughout our lives, there is also a bright and beautiful light that shines at the end of those dark and lonely tunnels. It is essential, not optional, that we keep faith as the main focus of our lives and remember that God will always show up on time.

Notes:

July 13

Is there a vast difference between what you say and what you do? Our word is, oftentimes, the only thing we have to offer. Once that word has no more validity, there's nothing left. Practice aligning your words and your actions. Be consistent in showing who you are.

I want to live up to your expectations of me, Lord. Teach me how to do things and when to do them. I want to be dependable and trustworthy. Show me where I fall short so that I can bring them to you for advice. Amen!

Notes:

July 14

Have you ever noticed when you smile, everything seems better, even if it's not? A smile says to the world, "I'm OK." It says that although things may be topsy turvy, "I am going to be OK." A smile really is worth a 1,000 words. Keep lighting up the rooms that you walk into.

Notes:

July 15

There is a significant distinction between leaders and followers. We must make the decision to lead or follow, so choose wisely. Make decisions based on what is best for you and where you are trying to go in life and not because you are blindly following someone. Doing the opposite of what you believe and feel is right. When we don't make decisions someone else will make it for us.

Notes:

July 16

No one said that trying to live our dreams was going to be easy. We will never know what could've been if we never step out and take a chance on ourselves. See all things new as an opportunity, an opportunity for growth and strength. I encourage you today to step out on faith and take a chance on yourself. Your dreams are just as important as anyone else's.

Notes:

July 17

There is a gospel song that goes a little like this: "In the hands of the Almighty, I've been set free, healed, delivered. I got my joy back." If you are someone who has lost your joy, I want to encourage you today to go find it back again. It's worth the fight and the sacrifice. What the world didn't give you, the world can't take away because Joy comes from the Lord, not man.

Notes:

July 18

No matter how bad things may look, or how bad they are, never give up. You are worth fighting for, so fight for your life. It is true what they say: "The Lord gives us no more than we can bear." But just when you think you can't take another thing, He sweeps in and pulls you up. Don't give up!

Dear Jesus, I want to learn to stop focusing on my circumstances and to place my trust and hope in you.. I want to be a person stands on your promises, even when I am unsure. AMEN!

Notes:

July 19

What we allow to enter our spirit, will be what is displayed outwardly. To have the best life possible, we must not only be accountable for the things we say and do, who we hang around, what we watch, and what we listen to. All of these things are within your control, and are decisions we must make. Making the correct or incorrect decision will have consequences.

Notes:

July 20

To seek happiness and wholeness in others, remember materialistic things, personas, activates, etc., will only provide a temporary fix. When we seek God, He will fill those voided areas in our lives so that we will become complete in Him. Submit yourself to God and let Him take care of the rest. Believe that whatever He has for you is better.

Notes:

July 21

Nobody enjoys doing things for people that never show appreciation. If we want more things in our lives, we must be appreciative of the things and the people we have in our lives. Have an attitude of gratitude today (and every day). Start your day with gratitude and end it with forgiveness so that your heart can replenish overnight to make space for more gratitude the following morning.

Notes:

July 22

In order to make a difference in our lives and the lives of those around us, we must, first, be different, and do something different. Our comfort zone never takes us anywhere that matters. If you're intimidated and scared stepping out and doing something new and different, it's a sure sign it is something you must do. Even if you don't trust yourself, trust the God that created you. You've got this!

Notes:

July 23

Not one of us has been untouched by grief, hurt, pain, or sorrow. It's never a question about what happens to us, it's about what you do when it does. What do you do when life slaps you in the face? We have a choice as to how we respond. We can fall prey to our circumstances, or we can get up, ask for the help we need, and hold tightly to God's everchanging hand. And I promise, you step-by-step, day by day, moment by moment, minute by minute, you will come through on the other side.

Notes:

July 24

The reason you are here today reading this devotional is because you didn't give up. Had you given up that time when the worst thing you thought could happen, did, you wouldn't have been able to experience the love and the light in your life today. You are where you are NOW because you didn't give up. Never stop striving to overcome life's ills because at the end of the day, it's about your purpose, not about your feelings.

Notes:

July 25

Who told you, you weren't good enough? Who said you couldn't? The real question is who are you paying attention to? It's not about what people say, it is your response to what they are saying. Do you remember being a kid and people calling you names? You would say, "I know you are but what am I?" Or something to that effect. Fact is, we shouldn't address every situation that comes our way.

Notes:

July 26

For every finger we point at others, there are just as many pointing right back at us. Be careful of the people whom you talk about, criticize, put down, and ridicule. You never know when the tables will turn and you may need that person. You never know if that person will be someone who can help you obtain something to save your life, or to help you in some way. We just never know. Since we are clueless to what God is doing, we should, at all times, act as though everyone is Jesus in disguise.

Notes:

July 27

There are times people will say things that hurt us to our core. But we know that that person only told us that because they love us and need us to know when we are out of line. There's a difference between people that tell you things out of love and people that tell you things out of malice. Anyone that loves you is going to come at you with love, those that don't love you, will come with malice.

Notes:

July 28

There is beauty all around us if we take the time to see it. There is the smell of sweet fragrances at every turn if we take the time to smell them. There is wonder all around us if we just take the time to look. We will never see the beauty of things that God has created unless we take the time to do so. Don't leave this world without taking time for people, for beauty, for nature, and last but not least, for God.

Notes:

July 29

How do you start your morning each day? Are you grateful that you were able to open your eyes? Are you grateful that you're able to stand on your own two feet? Are you thankful that you have the use of your bodily functions, organs, and limbs? Are you grateful for being in your right mind and able to read this message? Honey, there is always something to be thankful for. If you're unsure how to be thankful, just take a look around you. Take a look around because at the end of the day, you may not be where you would like to be, but baby, you are not where you used to be.

Notes:

July 30

Why are we so afraid to show that we don't know something? We sit back and have questions about a particular matter, but we don't ask the question. Why do we do that? It's absurd! The only way to get an answer is to ask the question. I guarantee that if you ask the question, whether you're in class, work or church, it will not only benefit you, but others as well. Everyone is hoping and praying someone else will ask the question, why not let it be you.

Notes:

July 31

I like parties just as much as the next girl, but a pity party looks good on no one. We can sit and feel sorry for ourselves all day and night, but it will not change one thing. Waddling in self-pity is tiresome for not only you, but for those that have that front row seat to it. We must pick ourselves up and keep moving forward. If the truth be told, the world will keep going regardless of the state of mind you are in. So, why not get yourself together and add your voice and gifts and talents to it.

Notes:

August 1

If anyone or anything causes you to be anything other than who you are, the cost is too high. People will try to change you because they feel intimidated by who you really are. Anyone that asks or tries to convince you to do anything contrary to your character and principles is not a good person to associate with. Stay focused on who you are and what you are here to do.

Notes:

August 2

There is an old saying that goes something like, "If your best isn't good enough, try, try again." Well, there may be times when your best isn't good enough and you need to do something different. It may not be totally on you, though. It could be because you are operating outside of grace, meaning you are in the wrong place. When we are not where we should be, things get out of whack really quick. Ask God if you are where you should be and if you feel strongly enough that His answer is no, ask Him to remove you.

Notes:

August 3

We must be intentional with our words. Once the message has been delivered, there is no coming back. Take a moment to think about what we want to relay, how we want it to sound, and the tone we will use to carry it. Your word is like an arrow, once cast, you can never take it back. Choose them wisely and with utmost care.

Lord Jesus, I will be the first to admit that I don't always use wisdom, especially when my emotions are high. Sometimes, I can be quick to speak and slow to think. Teach me oh Lord to decrese so that you will increase. AMEN!

Notes:

August 4

We can only meet people where they are and address them accordingly. No longer can we place everyone into the same box and give them the same solutions, because we all have different skills, strengths and weaknesses. Just as our personalities vary, our situations in life vary too. Therefore, it is a must that we be treated as such, individually.

Notes:

August 5

Be wary of people who always have something bad to say about others, especially when they are not around. This is toxic behavior and before you know it you will be chiming in on the comments, even about those you genuinely like. Toxicity is contagious, and if you are not careful, you will become a part of the problem and not the solution

Notes:

August 6

That grass in your neighbor's yard isn't always as green as it seems. Before we start lusting and coveting things that do not belong to us, we should understand the fact that what's for us is for us. We must settle in our spirit and be thankful and content for what we have and where we are currently. I am not saying this because I am in need, for I have learned to be content whatever the circumstances. 12 "I know what it is to be in need, and I know what it is to have plenty. I have learned the secret of being content in any and every situation, whether well fed or hungry, whether living in plenty or in want. 13 I can do all this through him who gives me strength." Philippians 4:11-13 (NIV)

Notes:

August 7

Are you preparing yourself for the blessings of God? We pray and ask God for this or that, but are you making room for these things? Sometimes, we need to spring clean our lives just as we do our homes so that we will have room for blessings when it comes. We can't expect God to bless our home if we are busy tearing someone else's down. Remember, a wise woman builds her home. A foolish woman tears it down with her own hands (Proverbs 14:1).

Notes:

August 8

Trouble always finds comfort where it is welcomed. But just because it knocks on the door doesn't mean you have to invite it in and make it feel at home. We have to take responsibility for the parts we play in our own dysfunction. We must also hold ourselves accountable for all the chaos that we create in our own lives.

Lord, help me to not only notice red flags and warning signs before heand, but to adhere to them. Equipt me with courage and boldness to say no and walk away from situations and people that are hazardous to my health and wellbeing,

Notes:

August 9

Our not making a choice regarding our peace, state of mind, and happiness is still a choice. We can't complain about the things we are not willing to change or willing to address. Sometimes, our biggest problem is us. As they say, indecision is a decision. Think next time before you leave a matter undecided, and act on it in time before it's too late.

Notes:

August 10

The reason our eyes are strategically placed in the front of our face is so that we can move forward. Living in the past keeps you bound to it. It does not allow for growth. Matthew 6:34 KJV states: "Sufficient for the day is its own troubles." Stay focused and live in the present, not the past or to-morrow.

Lord, Help me to focus on things that are in front of me and not behind me. Not only do I want to, I need to move forward in life, not backwards. Amen!

Notes:

August 11

Those that pray on the weaknesses and vulnerabilities of others can make you feel like you're in the wrong when the truth is that they are. Those type of people are predators, and they will do anything in their power to make you feel inferior to them. Don't fall for it. Keep your head high and defeat their purpose.

Notes:

August 12

The world is a perpetual circle that is constantly spinning. What we do in life, will come back to us. It's called reaping and sowing and the Law of attraction. If you want to have a fruitful life, be good to those you encounter. If you want more love, give love. If you want more time, give others your time. If you want more friends, be friendly. The things you want most are what you must be willing to give away because it will always come back to you.

Notes:

August 13

Each person who has ever left you could not stay, and those who stayed could not leave. Because nothing is wasted, each experience in life has something valuable to teach us. They will teach us all along the way. Wanting people to stay in our lives who need to leave is one of the worst things we can do. Recognize when someone's season has passed and let them go.

Notes:

August 14

When we insist on putting ourselves down and not valuing the person God has created us to be, it is like saying God was wrong. He was wrong in His choice of bestowing our beauty, personality, intelligence, and abilities. If you know nothing else, please know this: God does not make Mistakes. Every hair on your head is numbered and strategically placed there. Trust God, not man or even your own thoughts for that matter.

Notes:

August 15

What we allow will continue. If we let people walk over us, they will. We have to stand up with the boldness of the Lord and put people on notice that we are the daughters or sons of the King and will not remain in the presence of those who treat us any less than that. Keep your chin up and your head held high, you have earned it by being in the presence of the Lord.

Notes:

August 16

When you don't know which way to go or which way to turn, you just call on the name of Jesus and He will direct your path. God's plan is always the best plan, and I promise that if you seek Him, you will find Him. He asks for you to walk toward Him, and in doing so, you only make Him your biggest ally. Remember, if He is your ally, you don't need anyone else to be on your side.

Notes:

August 17

Not everyone is going to be good and kind to you because you are good. In today's world, it seems as though people no longer need a valid reason to be ugly; they just are. Hear me clearly. Don't allow the actions of people that behave badly to impede on your good heart and nature. You are responsible for the goodness of your heart, just as they are responsible for the ugliness of theirs.

Notes:

August 18

We must never allow temporary people to make decisions for your life that will have permanent consequences. Stand firm in your values and beliefs. Those that offer anything contrary to them are not for you. They are against you. Be steadfast in your prayers of guidance. And beware, because they will try their best to dissuade you from your path.

Notes:

August 19

Our world is changing at an epic rate and if you do not change with it, you will be left in the shadows of the past. Change is inevitable, and embracing change has the potential of being the greatest thing you will ever discover. So, open your mind, heart, and eyes, and step boldly into change. That is the only way to survive and thrive in this ever-evolving world.

Notes:

August 20

"Guilty by association" are the words no one wants to hear, but when we follow the wrong people down the wrong path, that could very well be where we end up. The kind of company we surround ourselves with matters and has an influence over us. People rub off their ways on us, but it is up to us to be our authentic self. Fight for your right to be unapologetically you.

Notes:

August 21

The reason your spouse and friends are individual people with their own minds, thoughts, and personalities is because they are the opposite of you. Frankly, I don't know if I could stand another me walking around. They are the yen to our yang. They complement our weaknesses and vice versa. So, love on them. Let them be who they are and you be who you are.

Notes:

August 22

Be sensitive to those that encounter your space and the spaces you encounter. There is a tremendous amount of fear, hurt, and anxiety these days, and the one thing we can do that will not cost anything, and with little effort, is to be kind to one another. Kindness spreads like a virus. If you are kind to one person every day, it will initiate a chain reaction which everyone will benefit from.

Notes:

August 23

You have the power within to accomplish everything that you have envisioned for yourself. The Lord has already gone before you and paved the way. You just have to believe you can walk the path He has set for you. "Trust in the Lord and lean not unto thine own understanding" (Proverbs 3:5-6 KJV).

Notes:

August 24

We are beautifully and wonderfully created by almighty God himself, so never allow others to tell you anything different. We must believe the word and not man. Man will tell you false truths about yourself and have you believing them. But God's word is forever (and faithful) (1 Peter 1:25 NKJV). You can count on that; you can always count on God.

Notes:

August 25

We have to let God be God in all situations. The reason something is not turning out the way you think it should is because the hand of God is not on nor in it. We go about our day doing things that we never ran by God. Then we wonder why certain things happen. Include Him in the smallest things in your life and He will show up and out.

Notes:

August 26

Each person we encounter should be left with the impression that God dwells inside of us. If anyone leaves our presence worse than when they came, we have a major problem. We should all do a self-assessment before we start speaking to others asking ourselves "is what I'm about to say adding to or taking away from this person or situation? Is what I have to say relevant and is it necessary? If not, say nothing at all.

Notes:

August 27

Looking for love in all the wrong places can and will, oftentimes, cause a lifetime of grief and destruction. If it is love you yearn for, go to the Father and pour your heart out to Him regarding your needs and wait on Him to send that special someone your way. Trust me, He will do just that. All you need to do is put your faith in God.

Notes:

August 28

The reason God has given us all two ears and one mouth is so that we listen more and talk less. If we are busy talking, how can we possibly hear what the other person is saying? We can't. The more we listen, the more we will learn. And by doing that, we are also able to listen to all the things that God wants us to hear. Try it; it really works.

Notes:

August 29

Why do we hold things in instead of addressing them? Some may say, "You are always arguing." Some may even say, "You always have something to say about everything." It is not what you say, it's the way you say it. The worst messages can be received well if it is done so from a place of compassion, concern, and love. Everything has a time and a place. Don't pass up the chance to address issues, which can be more of a hindrance in your life than the pain you're experiencing.

Notes:

August 30

Whatever it is you seek for your life and future, no matter how scary it appears, do it anyway. I know you're afraid but do it anyway. Find yourself some people that have been where you are trying to go and ask for help. I know you are scared to ask people for help but do it anyway! It's ok to be nervous, afraid, and anxious, but do it anyway. If you happen to fail at what it is you are trying to do, do it again, and again, and again, until you are no longer afraid. Then you will have mastered it.

Notes:

August 31

Learning to forgive those that have hurt you is one of the hardest things you'll ever do. But forgiving them is necessary in order for you to move forward uninhibited. Yes, we can still move forward if we don't forgive, BUT, you will move forward more freely if you do. Life is hard enough. Don't go through it with another person strapped to your back.

Notes:

September 1

There are people waiting and needing to hear what you have to say. We all have a voice, and we are to use it to the fullest. Silence the voices that are telling you, "Nobody wants to hear what you have to say. You are going to get up there make a fool of yourself." That is nothing more than the enemy trying to talk you out of what God has for you.

Notes:

September 2

From your struggle, you will find your strength. Nothing is wasted with God. That thing that you thought would be the thing to take you out, will be your greatest teaching tool. You will be able to not just show people how they, too, can rise from the ashes like a phoenix. You will be the walking, living proof that God is good.

Notes:

September 3

Isn't it funny how you can have someone with you all day, every day, and never fully appreciate them? Once people leave your life voluntarily or invol-untarily, their absence seems to suffocate you. We must start fully appreciating people when they are present. When someone's leave is voluntary, you may have the opportunity to make up for lost time. But when the leave is involuntary, you can't undo what has been done. You can't unring that bell. Make the most of each moment.

Notes:

September 4

Because tomorrow is not a promise, it is a must that we do what we need to do today. If you can do it later, you can do it now. Procrastination is just a fancy way of saying we are lazy, and at the end of the day, it is just that: lazy. It looks good on no one and can take hold of any of us if we allow it to. We must live each day as if it were our last because it may very well be just that.

Notes:

September 5

Yes, it is true. If you were not strong enough for the battle, you would not have been chosen to fight. The reason people lose in the battles of life is because they gave up on themselves. You've never seen a fighter that was in it to win it, up and quit. He fights because he knows that if he doesn't fight, he will have given the fight to his opponent. If you fight the other person, the message to them is, win or loose, I'm here for the fight.

Notes:

September 6

If we expect to be taken at our word, we must ensure our word is valid. No one is going to believe in someone who stretches the truth, exaggerates, and, frankly, lies day in and day out. Your word should have a value and should be considered believable. Mean what you say and say what you mean; if not, it's nothing more than hot air.

Notes:

September 7

Nothing is more intense and challenging than trying to love unlovable people. It's like trying to walk through a brick wall: the more you try to love them, the more they push you away. Unlovable people don't love themselves when they are in a state of chaos, therefore, it is impossible for them to embrace what you have to offer. It's not necessarily something that you've done. Sometimes, we are not someone else's answer.

Notes:

September 8

Not everyone is good or has good intentions. Some people are on assignment to wreak havoc and discord in your life. Identify them, keep them at arm's length, which is where they belong. Don't become angry and start tripping when they act out; they are only doing what they do. It's who they are. They are doing their part, and our part is to recognize it and stay clear.

Notes:

September 9

Good or bad, who we are innately will be present at all times. Trying to dumb down or putting up a façade is short lived. The true person should always present themselves. Just be you and those assigned to you will respond. Those that do not are not part of your assignment and that is ok. Just by being yourself, you will attract like-minded people and repel those who are not good for you.

Notes:

September 10

When you see people on the corner or on the me-dian with signs that say, "Hungry, need food. Please help." Do you give them money? Do you act as if you can't see them? No matter what you feel in your heart regarding their situation, if there is an urging in your spirit to help them, help them. If you don't have an urge to help, keep it moving. The conversation we have in our heads as to why they are there is really none of our business.

Notes:

September 11

I remember hearing this song when I was growing up that said something to the effect of, "If you can't be with the one you love, love the one you're with." Let me be the first to say, Ahhh... NO! Besides, that's gross! If you can't be with the one you love, dust yourself off and tell yourself, Put yourself on notice, you deserve someone who wants to spend time with you. The person that is out there searching for you will treat you as special as you are, and not like an in-convenience.

Notes:

September 12

The worst feeling in the world is to put off going to see or speak with someone and something happens to that person before you get another opportunity. We should never put off tomorrow what can be done today. Life will do what life loves to do which is to get in the way. So, make that call or schedule that visit today.

Notes:

September 13

When we look at our circumstances and where we are currently, it can look bleak and dismal. But when we look at all the possibilities and all the dreams and aspirations God has bestowed within us, we develop hope in our future and faith that it will present itself at the right time, at the right place, and with the right people.

Notes:

September 14

Paying excessive attention to everyone else's life and business and affairs is nothing short of nosiness and being a busybody, which is a negetive way of living. Take care of your to your own affairs, build yourself, and uplift others, rather than tearing people down. By turning that negetive energy into doing something good for others will render mind blowing rewards.

Notes:

September 15

Believing that our dreams are frivolous is like saying God doesn't know what He's doing. Our dreams can make us nervous because we don't know the outcome. But that is exactly why they are called dreams. Although we may not know if it will work out ok, God does. Trust His plan because His plan is the best you will ever have.

Notes:

September 16

Whatever it is in life you are believing for, can and will come to fruition. Everything starts and ends with what you believe. Positively or negatively, believe it and believe in it and you can achieve it. That is what the law of attraction states, you attract whatever you believe in. Believe in good and good shall happen to you. Believe in yourself, and you shall persevere.

Notes:

September 17

Some people will not only clutter your life, but they will also clutter your mind with negative and toxic rhetoric. Don't be a person that goes along to get along. What we allow will persist.

Lord, please send good and wholesome people into my life that I can be vulnerable and honest with. If there is anyone in my life that is not sent by you, remove and replace them. AMEN!

Notes:

September 18

Newton's third law states that for every action, there is an equal and opposite reaction. The decisions we make should take this law into consideration in order to adequately prepare for what will follow. Oftentimes, we make our decisions based on how we feeling the moment. When we consider the effects of our actions, we are more likely to make the best choices possible.

Notes:

September 19

If we can conceive anything, we can achieve it. Man didn't land on the moon because of an afterthought. He landed on the moon because the idea was not just a thought or a dream, but it was nourished and implemented. Nothing happens just because we thought about it. Our thoughs must be put into action. Many people perish daily with their thought and dreams still inside of them. So, think it and then do it.

Notes:

September 20

Be you at all costs because everyone else is already taken. God created you with your looks, your family, your gifts, and your talents, not for you to live out someone else's destiny. We must embrace all that encompasses who we are and know and believe that the plan for our life is one of awesomeness and not mediocrity.

Notes:

September 21

Many of us go through life doing things that are not in our wheelhouse of strengths and talents. The reason we don't seem to not flourish on our jobs is because we don't have grace for it. We are doing the wrong things. The reason our marriage is tumultuous is because we are married to the wrong person. The reason why it seems like we are running and getting nowhere fast is because we are operating against the grain not with it. Seek God, He will reveal your hidden gifts and talents as well as His plan and purpose for your life.

11 For I know the plans I have for you," declares the LORD, "plans to prosper you and not to harm you, plans to give you hope and a future. Jeremiah 29:11

Notes:

September 22

Be steadfast in all that you are and know to be true. You are right where you should be in this moment in time. For some, it is because of the choices of others. For others, it is because of their choices. Nevertheless, when you discover the why of who and what you are, you will have the answers you seek.

I am who and what I am not only because of things done to me by others, but most importantly, the things I have orchestrated myself in my search to give my life meaning. No matter how displaced, or destructive the end results.

Notes:

September 23

It is imperative that we embrace where we are currently and what we have. Take Inventory of all things and sit back, take it all in, and be thankful that while you may not be where you would like to be, by the grace of God, you are not where you were. We are all a work in progress, and each day is an opportunity to do better and be better.

Notes:

September 24

Hurt people have always and will always do just that, hurt other people. Until the hurt is acknowledged and addressed, the cycle will continue. Get free from the bondage that has held you captive all these years. It is not the life God has planned for you. Let go of the hurt and suffering and accept it as something God is using to make you stronger. Only then will you be able to move on.

Notes:

September 25

How to lose people quickly? Take them for granted, put them down, chip away at their vulnerabilities, shame them. People will ride with you as long as they think you care. Once you show them that you don't, you will lose them. What you say may be forgotten, but how you made someone feel will be remembered forever.

Notes:

September 26

"Ask and you shall receive, seek and you shall find," says Matthew 7:7. We like to make assumptions. If we want to know the answer, we must first ask the question. How will we know if we don't ask? We should not assume we know what people are thinking or what they're responses will be. More times than not, we are dead wrong.

Notes:

September 27

There is always someone in observance of you. Be exemplary in all that you do. It's just like keeping a clean house; if it's clean day in and out, you will never have to worry about company popping in and being unprepared. It's the same analogy that if you are always at your best, you'll never be caught off guard. Inspire people around you by being your best self today and every day.

Notes:

September 28

There is plenty to smile and be happy about. If you are reading this devotional, it's a blessing you can see. You woke up this morning, and that's a blessing. You see, there is so much to be thankful for and smile about. Because we tend to take things for granted, we just need to dig a little deeper to find it. Your reason to be happy today is there, just look for it.

Notes:

September 29

All any of us can do is take it one day and one step at a time. Life tends to be overwhelming and chaotic at times and we can't see the forest for the trees. Take it step by step (tree by tree) and before you know it, you will have covered and conquered your challenges (the entire forest). Small and firm steps will always help you be steady and cover more ground than big hasty steps.

Notes:

September 30

As human beings, it is natural for us to want what we want, even if it is not the best thing for us. But God's will is always sufficient and will render the best results possible. His will is always what is in our best interest. You wouldn't seek your mechanic for advice on health related issues would you? So, why would you lean on your own understanding regarding your life and circumstances when He is the author and finisher of life?

Notes:

October 1

Relevancy is the key to all things that keep us focused, balanced, and sane. We have to keep the important things in focus and not worry about the things that have no impact on the direction in which our life is headed. Stay centered. That is the only way to achieve all that you have put your mind to. Being centered and focused ultimately leads you to success.

Notes:

October 2

The worst crime and sin we commit is to leave this world with our gifts and talents still inside. Our life is not our own. Our existence is to do the will of God on this earth, which consists of helping and loving one another. Your gifts and talents will make room for you, but the grace of God will carry and sustain you where those gifts cannot.

Notes:

October 3

What good is it to overcome the storm and not help others to do the same? We must tell everyone we encounter about Jesus, His goodness, and all that He has done for us. There are people out there in the world with ears to hear your voice. You are the only one that can reach them, so you let your voice be heard. There is a time to be silent and a time to speak. Now is your time to speak.

Notes:

October 4

Givers give wholeheartedly and takers will take everything. Which one are you? It's never too late to turn negative actions into positive ones. We must make a conscious decision that our life is more than what we do for ourselves. It's not always easy looking at the woman or man staring in the mirror, but it's necessary.

Notes:

October 5

If you have any hopes and dreams for your future, it is pivotal that you be around people that will help develop and nurture them. Aspirations left unattended become distant memories. Just like what Langston Hughes says in his poem, A Dream Deferred, "Dreams can dry up like raisins in the sun". There are more people willing to help you flourish than there are not.

Notes:

October 6

We all have and will continue to encounter many different people throughout our lives. Some of them, we hope will never leave. Then there are some, we can't wait for them to leave. Get in the habit of consulting with God in all things. Ask Him what is it He is trying to teach or show you, because there are valuable nuggets in each aspect of our journey.

Notes:

October 7

Be mindful of what you speak over yourself and others. The reason there are so many broken people today is because death was spoken over them at some point. We must take full responsibility for the role we play in others' lives. When we come face to face with the Lord, we have to answer for our actions. Life and death are in the power of the tongue" (Proverbs 18:21).

Notes:

October 8

When we respect our planet, the planet gives us something in return. Clean energy, oxygen, beautiful flowers, rivers, oceans, and so on. When we inspire others, they will inspire us by living fruitful lives, discovering strengths within themselves, inspiring others, and so on. You see, everything you put out, will always come back to you. What we give, we get.

Notes:

October 9

Other people's opinion of you really does not have anything to do with you. It has everything to do with them. To not have an opinion about someone is one thing, but to possess the energy of dislike is a different ballgame. We should not give two cents about the opinions of others in relation to who we are. Let them dislike you all the way to a full and wonderful life.

Notes:

October 10

Life is going to continue moving forward re-gardless of your participation. The world doesn't stop spinning because of our feelings. So, we just need to pick ourselves up, dust ourselves off, and get over ourselves because life doesn't care about how we feel. The world goes on and so does life. Just because something bad happened shouldn't be a reason for us to stop living.

Notes:

October 11

Your voice has a purpose other than making noise. Yes, we all have something to say regarding one thing or another, but is it purposeful? Are your words impacting others negatively or positively? We must look beyond the surface of "it's only words," and be intentional in building up any and every one within the sound of our voice.

Lord God, enable the words I speak to bring life and love. Anything contrary to that, remove the utterance from my lips. I want the things I do any say to be pleasing in your sight and to those on the receiving end. AMEN!

Notes:

October 12

What is it that you believe? What is it that you are believing for? Is your belief system built on sinking sand or a solid foundation? Stand strong in your faith no matter what. When it feels like the walls are closing in, and you've lost your footing, take hold to the everlasting, ever-knowing, almighty God and believe within the depths of your soul that "all things work for the good of those that love Lord" (Romans 8:28).

Notes:

October 13

If we are not careful, people will hijack our emo-tional well-being. God gave us tears to flush out our emotions. Tears prevent emotional con-stipation. When you are emotionally constipated, your emotions and feelings run amuck. You have no stability, and you have no control over how to exhibit your emotions. So, let those tears flow. Free yourself.

Notes:

October 14

When people make you angry they are in control of your emotional state. If it were not so, they would not be able to anger you. We have to search within ourselves to find out why is it that we allow others to take us out of our best selves, and, in turn, seek a solution. A person that is easily angered is unstable in their ways.

Lord, help me to keep my cool in hot places. Help me to remain steady and planted in whatever circumstance that come my way. AMEN!

Notes:

October 15

One of the biggest mistakes we have all made is to make the statement, "I would never do that." It's easy to say what you wouldn't do if you are not faced with the actions that would cause a re-action. Someone once told me "Child, don't you ever say what you wouldn't do because cir-cumstances will have you doing some things you never thought you would." Be mindful of the words you speak and judging others. Let he who is without sin cast the first stone. (John 8:7 KJV).

Notes:

October 16

Until we take a hard look at the root of our negative actions, feelings, and words, nothing will change. Change starts with a mind shift. If once you start the process, nothing happens, push yourself and hold on to God, even if with one finger. If you take one step He will take two. The one thing you can depend on, is that God will be a constant source of all that you need in your life.

Notes:

October 17

How can we expect to receive and not give? Our world spins around and around, which is exemplary of what goes around comes around. It's a double-edged sword; closed palms can't give nor are they able to receive. Give with an open heart and watch the blessings that come to you in return. The Lord will never let your offering go in vain.

Lord Jesus, I know that a closed fist cannot receive, but sometimes it is difficult for me to give when all I see are my needs.

Notes:

October 18

Hearing and listening are two different things. It takes a concentrated effort to intently listen to what others have to say. How often do we actively pay attention to the words being relayed to us? A well informed person is always listening to what is being said. Keep your ears (and heart) open. Only then will you be able to receive the Lord's blessings completely.

Notes:

October 19

While complaining about everything, will sometimes get you the attention you seek momentarily, but it also pushes people away. No one likes being around Debbie Downers. If it appears people are shying away from you, there is usually a reason why. There is more to life than what's wrong within it. There is an abundance of things to be joyfully about. Find them and you will act accordingly.

Notes:

October 20

What God has for each of us is for us. The door the Lord opens cannot be shut, and the door the Lord closes cannot be opened. When you know of someone who is doing big things and is flourishing, you should celebrate them. Don't hate! Your day will come. There is enough of God's grace and favor to go around. It is enough for everyone that He has so beautifully created.

Notes:

October 21

What do you do when no-one is watching? Believe it or not, you are on someone's radar and they are keeping score. The biggest test of character comes when there is no audience. It's easy to pretend and put on a show when people are watching, but what do you do when it's just you left to your own accord. Never forget that even if no one is watching, God always is.

Notes:

October 22

Some of us have experienced bad times, unfairness, injustices, humiliations, and more. The good news is, we are not bound by what has happened to us. It is in the past for a reason. The enemy may have robbed you of past opportunities, but don't allow him to steal your future. Stay focused on God and the good things He is doing in your life right now.

Notes:

October 23

What we tolerate will persist. We may not have control over others, but what we do have control over ourselves. People who do not care about how you are feeling will do anything to you. Make the choice not to be in the presence of someone that makes a conscious decision not to care about your emotional well-being. Those people are like leeches, they suck you dry and then leave you once you no longer serve their purpose.

Notes:

October 24

When all we can do is muster up the strength to open our eyes, God will do the rest. Some things are our responsibility to fix. God's grace is sufficient for us all and He shows himself strong in our moments of weakness. If we could fix us, we would have done so. Give Him the wheel and allow God to do what you can't do for yourself.

Notes:

October 25

Unhappy people love making happy people un-happy. If you feel like the life is being sucked from you when you are around particular individuals, you need to sever all ties with them. You are important and allowing someone to invade your peace of mind is too high a price to pay. Let misery find company outside of you.

Notes:

October 26

It's natural to want people to like us and to want to fit in with our peers. Therefore, when we are rejected by those we want to be close to, it's devastating. The reason you are not accepted is because you were not meant to fit in. You, my friend, were meant to stand out. Be ok with that and know that God sends people to you. You do not need to chase them.

Notes:

October 27

Avoidance has never made the things we don't want to face vanish. Until we look the beast in the eye, we will forever be running. I know it's scary, intimidating, and it has you shaking in your boots at times, but the monster is never as big and as bad as we envision. Confront it and regain control and power over your life.

Notes:

October 28

Making assumptions about things we know nothing about can be hazardous to us. If you want to know something, ask. If you are not well informed, don't make assumptions. Get the facts before the facts get you. Once the damage has been, sometimes there is no coming back from that.

Lord, I don't want to go by what I think, but by what is true. Help me to not be swayed by what I hear, but in truth in truth alone. AMEN!

Notes:

October 29

Sometimes, a smile is worth a thousand words. When the weight of the world is on your shoulders, and it looks like there is no hope, by the grace of God, He allows you to cross paths with someone that captivates you with their infectious smile. This is the presence of God telling you He's got you. This is how hope can sometimes come to the weary from a simple smile.

Notes:

October 30

When we spend more time focusing on the good in our lives, the better our perception of it. There is an enormous amount of chaos to deal with day in and day out; we don't need to add to it by putting ourselves down because we missed a deadline. Be patient with yourself. You deserve the same grace you give yourself.

Notes:

October 31

What are you doing consistently that is moving you forward? We should be doing something each day that is moving us into the direction of our goals, visions, and aspirations. Anything outside of that is a waste of time, and time is something we can no longer afford to spare. Time is of essence and those who do not respect it are left behind to mourn it.

Notes:

November 1

Eventually, everyone gets tired. Then we get to the point where we want to throw in the towel on our jobs, relationships, marriage, even our children from time to time. Even animals get tired, yes animals. There is only so much any of us can take. Discovering the gift of saying no and goodbye is a lifesaving tool if utilized in an orderly fashion, so use it wisely and with care.

Notes:

November 2

If you want to make a difference in the world, do something for someone that has no way of repaying you. Just like loaning money to a family member, knowing they most likely will not pay you back. Yes, like that. Try helping someone who can't help you back, who can't reciprocate your generosity, who can't help themselves and the reward itself will be worth everything.

Notes:

November 3

We cannot be the solution to everyone's problems. We only need to be supportive, which encompasses prayer, love and comfort. We are not the solution to all the world's issues. Once we stop our God-like complexes, then and only then will we live more fulfilling lives by not trying to fight battles that are not ours to fight.

Notes:

November 4

"It is better to have loved and lost than to have never loved at all," said Alfred Lord Tennyson. Is it though? As I think about the many heartaches and heartbreaks I've endured, I have often thought to myself about the what ifs, the should haves, could haves, and would have's. But, yes, it is better to have loved because there were some good memories made. There were some valuable lessons learned and some wonderful relationships that were created.

Notes:

November 5

It has been said, that people who did not have a mother, father, or both actively involved in their lives search for that missing piece of the puzzle elsewhere. The search to fill that void may sometimes manifest in the form of rebellion, anger, resentment, promiscuity, drug abuse, drug dealing domestic violence, and other negative actions. The only way to fill an internal void of the heart and soul is through Jesus. I promise you if it is love you seek, you will find it in Him. If it is acceptance you crave, you will only find it in Him. If it is deliverance you need, through Him you can and will be free. Whatever the void, just try my Jesus.

Notes:

November 6

What is it that sets your soul on fire? What is it that you wake up thinking about and is also the last thing you think of before you lay down to sleep? What is the thought that intimidates you? What is the thought that makes you feel inadequate? What do you dream about that you feel you don't deserve or are not equipped to accomplish? Yes, those thoughts and dreams can be scary and downright terrifying, but do it anyway.

Notes:

November 7

We must all do what is required and necessary of us. Eventually, we will come to a place where those necessary things will become optional. We need Jesus continuously at every turn because He has already gone before us making a way when there was no way. There is nothing I would rather do without you, Lord. I require your assistance at all times. Please forgive me for leaving you out of my plans. I don't want to do it if you're not in it. I thank you Lord, for never forgetting me, even when I forgot about you.

Notes:

November 8

Futures can be told by the character of the people you hang around most frequently. If you are easily influenced by those you spend time with. Evaluate and take inventory of the affect the relationship is having on you. If it is a positive influence, you are on the right track. If it is a negative influence a purging of the relationship is necessary immediately.

Notes:

November 9

The United States Military is a prime example of bravery. While at times our soldiers may be intimidated and even afraid of the unknown, the mission is greater than the emotions they may be experiencing. Protect and serve at all costs is their job. Individually, they may not be able to withstand, but shoulder to shoulder and side by side, as a unit, their strength combined makes anything possible. Be bold in your faith and what you believe in, just like the military. Singularly, you may not withstand, but with the unity of other believers nothing is impossible.

Notes:

November 10

Your life, dreams, aspirations, goals, and most importantly, you, matter. Each morning when you open your eyes, thank God for blessing you with another day and then ask him for guidance. When you put God first, your dreams, aspirations, and goals will fall in line. Make putting God first, the the first thing you do every day.

Lord, I don't want to forget about you, but if I am being honest, sometimes I do. With all the noise and distractions in my life I sometimes put other things before you. Teach me prioritization Lord, so that I will always keep the main thing the main thing, which is YOU. AMEN!

Notes:

November 11

Let us strive to be better and do better. There is always room for improvement in our lives, regardless of how good we perceive ourselves to be. We all fall short of perfection. Asking for guidance and wisdom daily is guaranteed to change your world and transform you into a better version of yourself. Make the choice to do better, daily.

Notes:

November 12

If you are feeling like an outsider looking in, per-haps you are. You were created to stand out, not blend in. Once you have embraced this reality, you will find your place, and the people assigned to you will show up. Go out there and stand out on your own. Believe in yourself and the fact that you don't need anyone else's light to shine.

Notes:

November 13

It's not always easy trying to convince people to buy into your hopes and dreams as you chase after them. It can also be disruptive to someone that is accustomed to you being the person they've been used to. This doesn't not make them bad people, but it should make you think twice about who you bring into the next chapter of your life and who you will have to leave behind.

Notes:

November 14

Nothing around us will change if we do not change! To change the world, we must first change Our-selves. It is not always easy to admit this to our-selves and others. However, it is the most honest and revealing thing we can ever do. Nothing happens by pretending nothing happened. Be the first to become what you want the world around you to become, and watch it change like you wanted.

Notes:

November 15

When we don't find a way to help others in need, we fail. Helping is not always financial. It can be caring, supporting, love, mentoring, training, and so on. While money is necessary, it is not all that is needed. There are many people in need of emotional support in the world today. The more kindness and goodness you give to God's people, the more of the same you will receive from God himself.

Notes:

November 16

We can all become better people by doing better. It is not rocket science to treat others kindly. No degree is necessary to help someone in need. It is not a foreign language to show compassion. If you wish to become better, just be better and it is guaranteed to happen. The Lord will see to it that you receive His blessings in abundance, when you are good to others.

Notes:

November 17

What mistake we don't learn, we repeat. There are learning opportunities in each hard thing we endure if we are humbled enough to receive what the experience has to offer. To have to repeat the same mistake over and over again has the potential to be devastating, so learn the lesson the first time and keep it moving.

Notes:

November 18

If you couldn't handle the storm in your life, you wouldn't be facing it. Yes, it is hard and at times it can feel like it will be the end of you. But eventually, you will beat the thing that is beating you. Just keep standing. Hold onto the one that got you started in the first place, Jesus. It is a test, and He wants you to succeed in it, otherwise He wouldn't have sent it your way.

Notes:

November 19

Most of the time, the things we feel like we can't live without are the very things we take for granted, push aside, and neglect. Developing a deep appreciation for the things we have been blessed with is also an appreciation to God for His blessings. Life in itself is the biggest blessing to us from God. Don't waste it or take it for granted. Use it to do and be better every day.

Notes:

November 20

You were created to do great things in the world. Gifts and talents were instilled in you by God for His purpose before you were born. Even if you don't believe in yourself and your abilities, believe in God and that all things work together for those who love and believe in Him. Your belief is what brings you closer to God's love.

Notes:

November 21

Have you ever wanted something that you not only knew wasn't good for you, but also wasn't good to you? As human beings, we yearn to be connected to others, sometimes by any means necessary. We will take mistreatment, abuse, and degradation as long as we don't have to be alone. I'm here to tell you that is no way for you to live. Truth be told, you can do bad all by yourself. No one needs help in that area. You are better than the way you allow others to treat you.

Notes:

November 22

If it doesn't sit right in your spirit, God is trying to reveal to you something is off with a situation or person. I like to call them nudges from God telling us to fight or flee, speak or be silent, move or stand still, or leave or stay. If you are not in tune with your gut feelings, do so immediately by asking God how to tap into your intuition. It will save you from more trouble you can't get out of, and more heartache than you would want to endure.

Notes:

November 23

Words unspoken are never heard. So, why would you think someone should know how you are feeling at any given time? Healthy dialogue is the best way to start and end any conversation. When the dialogue is healthy, you can agree to disagree and respect can be rendered on both sides. Healthy dialogue allows you to here the other person's point of view, even if the view is skewed. Peace of mind is everything, and convincing someone who believes they are always right, that they are wrong never results in a peaceful dialogue.

Notes:

November 24

Take the time to take care of yourself. Running around doing everything for everyone else and not tending to your own business is insane. To be fully present in your quest to save the world requires you to be your best. Granted, some things are out of your control, and you will have to work with what you have, but for those things within your control that can be tweaked, why not?

Notes:

November 25

We are our greatest hindrances. We can do anything we set our minds to. We are who we say we are, and we can have what we claim we can have. Never mind what people say about you; the greater question is, what do you say about yourself, and most importantly, what does God say about you? Stop focusing on unimportant people and redirect your attention to God.

Notes:

November 26

To turn your ordinary into extraordinary, you must do some things ordinary people do not do, and that is to continually work on building yourself. When you keep learning, growing, and believing you can and you will. It is not everyone's destiny to achieve greater heights, but to those who work for and believe in a merciful God, it is available for the taking.

Notes:

November 27

What are you willing to do to have the life you imagined for yourself and your family? A dream is only a dream until you believe in it. We can't expect others to believe in our dreams if we don't. We can't expect others to believe in us if we don't.

Lord, help me to have faith in my abilities and gifts. You have bestowed upon me gifts and talents, which I intend to fully utilize. I don't want to be ashamed and afraid when it's time to move on. Give me the courage and strength to live the life you've planned for me.

Notes:

November 28

The best way to avenge yourself with your foes is to persevere and win. Each time you fail, get back up, come back harder and stronger and you'll win. If you don't, they win and you lose. When you fall, keep in mind that if it were easy, everyone would do it. The road to success is frequently lonely and fraught with negativity and skeptics.

Notes:

November 29

Be specific and intentional with the people you allow into your circle. Every smiling face isn't friendly, all pleasantries aren't always pleasant, and every open arm is not always welcoming. Pay attention to the little things people do and say because they are always displaying glimpses of who they are and their intentions.

Lord Jesus, I want to believe those around me have my best interest at heart. However, I fully aware that is not always the case. Help me to decern truth from lies so that I may purge my circle as needed.

Notes:

November 30

Love yourself enough to walk away from anything that threatens your values and your self-worth. Anyone that does not know how to treat you doesn't deserve one iota of your time; tell them to just keep it moving right out the front door. You don't need that kind of vibe around you. Do not surround yourself with such people as they will only bring you down.

Notes:

December 1

Don't allow yourself to become a punching bag for those that are miserable with their self-worth or lack thereof. Hurt people will lash out and take their frustrations out on anyone in their paths. Make every effort to move out of the way, and don't let them walk all over you. Because they were mistreated, they do not have the right to treat you in this manner.

Notes:

December 2

The reason we have what we have, is because of the grace, favor, and mercy. It is not that we are so great, but rather God is great. Your source, is in and always will be, in Him and Him alone. Our skills and our jobs are provisions He has allowed.

Thank you Lord, for everything you've done for, in, and through me. Thank you for the life you have given me. Thank you for seeing past my flaws and re-cognizing my needs. AMEN!

Notes:

December 3

If you can barely stand your attitude and behavior, what do you think everyone else's perception of you will be? Change what you need to change and move on. You will become a much better person for it. No one want to deal with a bad attitude. Working on yourself and identifying your shortcomings, is the recipe for success.

Lord Jesus, I know you, of all people, are aware that I, yes, I, can be a total mess and a handful. Help me tame the lion within me so that I can be a breath of fresh air in a sea of confusion and conflict. AMEN!

Notes:

December 4

Never let the opinions of others define you or dictate who and how you will be. People can be cruel and make you feel worthless. Go to God with your concerns and your fears, and he will transform you from the inside out, showing you who you are.

Lord, I don't want to worry about what people think about me. Help me tune the world out and tune into you. AMEN!

Notes:

December 5

Stay the course. No one ever did anything of substance by quitting. Those who quit never discover who they could have been. If it were not attainable for you, you would never have encountered it. Have faith that if God has placed it in your path, it is meant for you. Don't shy away from it. Persevere.

Notes:

December 6

Why do we get upset at people for just being who we know they are? Our wanting and wishing they were anything contrary is pure unadulterated fantasy. People will not veer far from who they genuinely are, so trust what you see and what you hear. If someone tells you they are crazy, believe them, because guess what? They are just that, crazy.

Notes:

December 7

In a hurry, too many things can and will go wrong. I've seen countless drivers rush through traffic only to end up a car or two ahead of where they started, or worse, cause an accident. A hurried anything often leaves room for the unexpected and, occasionally, disaster.

Lord, I know I rush things at times, making bad situations worst. Show me how to slow down and to take my time in all things. AMEN!

Notes:

December 8

We transform into something every time we consume anything that stimulates us, whether negatively or positively. What we allow on the inside will show up on the outside. We need to become aware of our own limitations, strengths, and weaknesses. When we become more self-aware, we become more sensitive to things that either help or hinder our growth and destiny, ultimately transforming us.

Notes:

December 9

If you are the person that knows unlimited information regarding unlimited topics, what are you learning from others? There should not be a day that goes by where we do not learn something new. Life is full of wonder and marvelous things. Take a seat at the students'desk and there is no doubt you will walk away informed. There is always something new to learn from those who are eady and willing to listen.

Notes:

December 10

Emotions and feelings have placed more people in comprising positions than we can ever imagine. We should remove our emotions from all major decisions to make the most informed decisions possible. Don't let your heart come inbetween the decision that your head knows is right for you. Being ruled by emotions is a path to distruction.

Notes:

December 11

Our failures will inspire others to keep pushing. They are encouragers for those that are currently walking the path you have already traveled. This is why we must keep going. Others need to see that we have made it so that they will know they can as well. Be the inspiration you wished for when you started the journey.

Notes:

December 12

We must decide that no matter the circumstances, we will be content. We will take the good with the bad, change what we can and pray about everything in between. Being content is hard to acheive, but it is also a path toward gratitude.

Lord, you know the path I take before the thou ght enters my mind. You are aware of my attitude s in situateions before they become visible. Assist me in bringing you glory through my attitude, re-actions, and responses. I only want what it is that you want from and from me.AMEN!

Notes:

December 13

Conflicting beliefs (dream killers) allow us to believe that regardless of how beautiful we are, we are not pretty enough. No matter how talented we are, we are not good enough. No matter how good a person we are, we don't deserve better. Today we change those beliefs. You are beautiful, you are good enough, and you deserve the best. Speak it and believe it.

Notes:

December 14

It can be disheartening to do all you can for those you love and care about and they don't seem appreciative. It can sometimes make you feel used and taken advantage of. Expectation, when it doesn't measure up, can and will break your heart. Beware of it. Remind yourself that your actions are what define you and theirs is what define them.

Notes:

December 15

Our failures serve as a motivating factor for others. They serve as a source of inspiration for those who are attempting the same journey you once traveled. This is what we need to keep going. It's important for others to see you made it, so that they can too.

Jesus, I can't do anything without you. You know what lies before and behind me. Help me to look to you. I can't accomplish anything without you, Jesus. Help me to focus on you rather than situations. There are people who require the services I provide, so I must see this through. Jesus, please help me. AMEN!

Notes:

December 16

Change what you think about daily and your world will change. When we are fixated on negatives, negatives will show up throughout our life. When we are fixated on positives, Jesus and his goodness, He will show up throughtout our life. Choose wisely daily to make your life what you want it to be.

Lord, give me positive thoughts as a template for my days and my nights. I trust you above all others and I know if my thoughts come from you, they will propel me.

Notes:

December 17

Optimism in regard to anything, comes easy because it's embedded within our DNA. It's who we are, it exudes from us. Negative people will do everything in their power to keep you from being optimistic; don't let them. If the people you associate with are pulling you down rather than pulling you forward, it is time to reconsider those relationships.

Notes:

December 18

Hanging onto hurt, disappointment, and unforgiveness manifests into anger, bitterness, and lonliness. Release it, and it will set you free. We can't joyfully and successfully go through life harboring offenses and unforgiveness because it kills and wreaks havoc in our lives. Let it go so that you can grow, both as a person and spiritually.

Notes:

December 19

God always sends us signs to confirm our destiny. We cannot become something we are not but we sometimes try. Who we are shows up in all stages of our lives from children to adults. We have only the grace to be who we are, nothing more and nothing less. Go out and be the best you that you can be.

Notes:

December 20

If we think about nothing, guess what? We become nothing. We are a sum of what we think daily. If we think of becoming anything, guess what? We can and will become anything. Think change, and you will become the change. If you think you are a loser, a loser it is. Don't take my word for it; try it for yourself. You attract what you speak.

Notes:

December 21

Over 7,000 deaths occur daily on average. It is no coincidence you were not one of them. You are alive today because your work is not yet completed. Arise with purpose each day. No matter how you are currently feeling in your body and spirit, you still have a purpose. Seize the day! "This is the day that the Lord has made, I will rejoice and be glad in it" (Psalm 118:24).

Notes:

December 22

I've heard it said time and time again, follow your heart; but should we, really? The heart can be de-deceiving, making you think something that is not true. The heart will tell you someone hits you because they love you. Your heart will tell you that a person who lies and cheats is the one for you. The heart will have you loving someone who does not love you back. Be mindful that the heart can be misleading.

Notes:

December 23

One of the greatest challenges we face, is getting out of our own way. At times, we are our own worst enemies. We know the right things to do, yet we do the opposite. Although our actions have the potential to cause us to self-destruct, we move forward. We know if we do this or that, it may hurt others, and we do it regardless. Change always start with us.

Notes:

December 24

It is a must that we discover the gift of saying no. It is good to be able to help and give back to whatever is giving to you. However, it is a must that we learn that we cannot be all things to all people all the time. When you are overworked and have fallen ill from exhaustion, someone else will take your place and you will be forgotten. We all need time to catch our breath, and if others can't and won't recognize that, we have to.

Notes:

December 25

To be constantly stressed out, worried about this or that, and afraid of everything, is no way to live and it's not God's plan or purpose for us. Not possessing the bandwidth to be at ease and relaxed due to being on the edge is not living; it is existing. Learn to relax, breathe; let the chips fall where they may, and let things be what they are so that you can live a life fulfilled.

Notes:

December 26

Stop making other people's problems your problems. It is one thing to have compassion for others and to help them, but it's something different when we allow the energies and negativity of others to infect us. All we can do is try to help others, but we can't want something for someone else more than they do. If someone wants something bad enough, they will fight for it.

Notes:

December 27

Who and what are you giving your attention to? If the attention and focus we willingly give away is not conducive to where we are headed, we are wasting valuable time that will never come again. When we finally get a clue, then and only then, we will know what to do. Be wise in who and what you spend your time and energy on.

Notes:

December 28

No matter what we go through, God always provides. Just as we sleep when we are tired, we wake when we have rested. Once we are refreshed and renewed, our perspectives change. This is why major decisions and discussions should never be made under duress. Sleep on it; marinate over it. Only then will we be equipped to address the elephant in the room.

Notes:

December 29

There will never be the perfect time for anything. Waiting until the time is just right never works. Now is the time to do whatever it is you need to do. Step outside of your comfort zone and do it now. If not, you will forever be waiting for the right time and it will never come. Don't miss your window because one day may be too late.

Notes:

December 30

Be well informed. To struggle and have doubts regarding truth and falsehoods is foolish. Get informed. The devastation that surrounds gossip can drastically effect someone elses life, specifically if what is being said is untrue. By the time word of mouth gets back to the originator, the story has drastically changed. Just as there is no honor among thieves, there is no confiding among busybodies. When we have the urge to interject ourselves into the middle of someone else's business, we must be well informed.

Notes:

December 31

We all have that special something that God placed inside of us way before our birth. If you are unaware of what your gifts are, I beg of you to find someone like your paster or spiritual leader that can help you find the answer. God's words say to knock and the door will be opened. Seek and you will find. Look inside yourself and you will discover what God had already put inside of you.

Lord Jesus, send people my way who can help me develop everything you've put inside of me. Teach me when and where to use my abilities and talents. Give me the guidance I need to become everything I was meant to be. AMEN!

Notes:

www.ingramcontent.com/pod-product-compliance
Lightning Source LLC
Chambersburg PA
CBHW050441150626
46551CB00028B/787